DAILY GRAMS: Guided Review Aiding Mastery Skills

for

4th & 5th

Grades

Author:
Wanda C. Phillips

Published by **ISHA Enterprises, Inc.**

Post Office Box 12520

Scottsdale, Arizona   85267

© 1987

ISBN   0936981-06-7

<u>DEDICATION</u>

DAILY GRAMS: GUIDED REVIEW AIDING MASTERY SKILLS FOR GRADES FOUR AND FIVE IS DEDICATED WITH LOVE TO MY WONDERFUL HUSBAND, JIM. THE PRIVILEGE OF SHARING HIS LIFE IS AN HONOR AND A BLESSING.

DAILY GRAMS: GUIDED REVIEW AIDING MASTERY SKILLS for 4th & 5th GRADES is designed as a guided review. There are 180 "**GRAMS**" in this book, one review per teaching day. **DAILY GRAMS** will take approximately **10 minutes** total time; this includes both doing and grading.

PROCEDURE:

1. Students should be **trained** to do "**GRAMS**" immediately upon entering the classroom. Therefore, "**GRAMS**" should be placed on the chalkboard or on an over-head projector.

2. Students will finish at different rates. Two ideas are suggested:

    A. Require students to have a reading book with them at **all times**. Students simply read when finished.

    B. Allow students "Three Minute Conversations" when they have completed **DAILY GRAMS.** Students will select a partner and discuss anything (within limits of school suitability). The requirement is that all thoughts are expressed in **complete** sentences. Those who work faster get the entire three minutes while others may only have a minute or two. The purpose, however, is that everyone is ready to check "**GRAMS**" at the same time.

3. Go over the answers orally with the entire class. In making students accountable for this type of activity, you may wish to take a quiz grade occasionally.

The purpose of <u>**DAILY GRAMS: GUIDED REVIEW AIDING MASTERY**</u> <u>**SKILLS - for FOURTH AND FIFTH GRADES**</u> is to provide students with **daily** review of their language. Bringing this information to the 'forefront' of one's memory will help to insure **mastery learning.**

FORMAT

You will note that each page is set up in this manner:

1.   Sentence one will always contain **capitalization** errors. Encourage students to write only the words that should be capitalized.

2.   In sentence 2 of each exercise, students will insert needed **punctuation.** It is suggested that students write out this sentence, adding proper punctuation.

3.   Both sentences 3 and 4 will be **general review.** You may want to replace one of these items with material you are currently studying.

4.   Sentence 5 is always a **sentence combining.** Using sentences given, students will write one, more intricate sentence. This helps the student move to higher levels of writing. If you feel that the sentences given are too difficult for your level, simply delete parts. You have been given two possible answers. Needless to say, there are more.

SUGGESTIONS

1. It is suggested that **"GRAMS"** be transferred to transparencies, numbered, and filed. In using them over a period of years, one only has to draw the **"GRAMS"** from the file.

2. The blackboard may also be used.

3. Some teachers will want to make copies for each student.

4. Solicit as much **student response** as possible.

5. If possible, allow students to write sentence combining on the board. Use this for class "editing" and **praise**!

6. As one progresses through this book, some of the sentences become longer and more complex. This may necessitate an adaptation to your own teaching needs.

STUDENT RESPONSE TO **DAILY GRAMS**

"**Grams** helps me to get my mind going when I get to English class."

"I'm learning about sentence combining."

"I really enjoy **Grams**. I think that they keep the material we have learned in our heads."

"They help me to remember things that I forgot."

"I really like **Grams**. I think they are fun, and we can learn from them."

"I think **Grams** helps me to remember everything we've learned."

CAPITALIZATION:

1. have dr. and mrs. c. winston visited new york?

PUNCTUATION:

2. Jill are you going

PARTS OF SPEECH: NOUNS

 Write the possessive form:

3. a balloon belonging to a child

SUBJECTS / VERBS:

 Underline the subject once and the verb twice.

4. Suddenly Janet sneezed.

SENTENCE COMBINING:

5. The pen is yellow.
    The pen is on the table.

DAY 2

CAPITALIZATION:

1. their school is on elm street.

PUNCTUATION:

2. No dont go

PARTS OF SPEECH: VERBS

Give the proper contraction:

3. A. is not
   B. they are
   C. cannot

SENTENCE TYPES:

Determine the type of sentence:

4. Are you leaving?

SENTENCE COMBINING:

5. The fly is on the ceiling.
   The fly is black.

CAPITALIZATION:

1.   the parade will start at fairmont school on birk lane.

PUNCTUATION:

2.   Wow I won

SUBJECTS / VERBS:

   Underline the subject once and the verb twice:

3.   A band marches every morning.

SENTENCE TYPES:

   Determine the type of sentence:

4.   A. Will you go?
      B. The sun is bright.

SENTENCE COMBINING:

5.   Mark is sick today.
      Mark had to stay home.

DAY 4

CAPITALIZATION:

1.   my aunt lives in san diego, california.

PUNCTUATION:

2.   Tom can you play

PARTS OF SPEECH: ADJECTIVES

3.   <u>A</u>, <u>an</u>, and <u>the</u> are special adjectives called _____.

PARTS OF SPEECH: VERBS

   Underline the subject once and the verb twice:

4.   Our dog licks us.

SENTENCE COMBINING:

5.   The basket is broken.
       The basket is green and pink.

CAPITALIZATION:

1.   did sandy move to prince street?

PUNCTUATION:

2.   Sue Frank and Lil were first

SUBJECTS / VERBS:

  Underline the subject once and the verb twice:

3.   Your chain fell on the floor.

PARTS OF SPEECH: ADVERBS

  Select any adverb(s) that tell <u>how</u>:

4.   She did her work carefully.

SENTENCE COMBINING:

5.   The telephone rang.
      Ted answered it.

DAY 6

CAPITALIZATION:

1.   last sunday nancy drove to austin, texas.

PUNCTUATION:

2.   He was born on Oct 20 1980

PARTS OF SPEECH: ADVERBS

   Select any adverb(s) that tell <u>when</u>:

3.   Today is our picnic.

PARTS OF SPEECH: PRONOUNS

   Select the correct pronoun:

4.   Bill and _____ (me, I) are right.

SENTENCE COMBINING:

5.   Debbie's bike had a flat tire.
        Debbie fixed her flat tire.

CAPITALIZATION:

1.	last christmas susan's family went to hawaii.

PUNCTUATION:

2.	Mary have you been to Denver Colorado

PARTS OF SPEECH: ADVERBS

Select any adverb(s) telling <u>where</u>:

3.	A child fell down.

SENTENCE TYPES:

Select the sentence type:

4.	A. Sit down.
	B. The ribbon was loose.

SENTENCE COMBINING:

5.	The dish was dropped.
	The dish broke into many pieces.

DAY 8

CAPITALIZATION:

1.   in august they visited the grand canyon in arizona.

PUNCTUATION:

2.   Dear Ben

       Ill meet you soon

             Your friend
             Mickey

PARTS OF SPEECH: CONJUNCTIONS

3.   The three (coordinating) conjunctions are _____, _____, and _____.

PARTS OF SPEECH: ADJECTIVES

 Select any adjective(s) telling <u>how many:</u>

4.   Several cats lapped milk.

SENTENCE COMBINING:

5.   Joe's mom is a dentist.
       Joe's dad is a dentist.

CAPITALIZATION:

1. has mrs. jones read <u>summer of the monkeys</u> to your class?

PUNCTUATION:

2. Anaheim California is the home of Disneyland

PARTS OF SPEECH: ADJECTIVES

  Select any adjective(s) telling <u>which one</u>:

3. Did you paint this picture?

SUBJECTS / VERBS:

  Underline the subject once and the verb twice:

4. That horse chews hay.

SENTENCE COMBINING:

5. The roses were blooming.
   The daisies were not blooming.

DAY 10

CAPITALIZATION:

1. was george washington's home called mount vernon?

PUNCTUATION:

2. Marge Frank and Miriam left early

PARTS OF SPEECH:

  Select the correct word:

3. (There, Their) dad is a carpenter.

SUBJECTS / VERBS:

  Underline the subject once and the verb twice:

4. Those trees sway in the wind.

SENTENCE COMBINING:

5. Jason mailed a letter.
    He did it for Dad.

CAPITALIZATION:

1.   dear terry,

        i will be there in june.

                  your friend,
                  tony

PUNCTUATION:

2.   Mary is coming at 10 15 A M

PARTS OF SPEECH: VERBS

  Give the contraction:

3.   A. should not   C. he will   E. I have
         B. are not   D. I am   F. will not

PARTS OF SPEECH: ADJECTIVES

4.   The three articles that will always be adjectives are _____,
        _____, and _____.

SENTENCE COMBINING:

5.   The chalkboard was dusty.
        Two students washed it.

DAY 12

CAPITALIZATION:

1.   the family of dr. kolb visited saddle river, new jersey.

PUNCTUATION:

2.   Mrs Tate doesnt have a marker

PARTS OF SPEECH: ADJECTIVES

  Select any adjective(s) telling <u>what kind:</u>

3.   Cold sandwiches and chocolate cake were served.

SUBJECT / VERBS:

  Cross out prepositional phrase(s). Underline the subject once and the verb twice.

4.   The bus with flashing lights stopped.

SENTENCE COMBINING:

5.   Jane's brother is on the swim team.
       Jane's brother is ten years old.

CAPITALIZATION:

1.　on monday we celebrated memorial day at a park.

PUNCTUATION:

2.　My aunts graduation was June 10 1987

PARTS OF SPEECH:

Select the correct word:

3.　(There, Their) are fifty pennies here.

PARTS OF SPEECH:　ADJECTIVES

Select any adjective(s) telling <u>how many:</u>

4.　A few squirrels gathered twenty nuts.

SENTENCE COMBINING:

5.　A carriage was pulled by a horse.
　　The carriage was decorated with flowers.

DAY 14

CAPITALIZATION:

1.   on saturday we will visit heard museum on palm lane.

PUNCTUATION:

2.   Our troop wont leave until 7 00 P M

PARTS OF SPEECH: ADJECTIVES

  Select any adjective(s) telling <u>what kind</u>:

3.   Big blue balloons were hanging there.

PARTS OF SPEECH: VERBS

4.   There are 23 helping (auxiliary) verbs. Name as many as you can.

SENTENCE COMBINING:

5.   Wendy plays on a softball team.
      Wendy plays first base.

CAPITALIZATION:

1.   the smith family lives at 22 east ball street, reno, nevada.

PUNCTUATION:

2.   No I did not read Blubber*

      *name of book

PARTS OF SPEECH: PRONOUNS

  Select the correct pronoun:

3.   A rooster chased _____ (I, me).

PARTS OF SPEECH: PREPOSITIONS

  Select the prepositional phrases in the sentence:

4.   After the movie we ate supper at a diner.

SENTENCE COMBINING:

5.   Ken skied for two hours.
      Ken fell three times.

DAY 16

CAPITALIZATION:

1.   matt's savings account is at thunderbird bank on bell road.

PUNCTUATION:

2.   One half of the birds arent flying

PARTS OF SPEECH: NOUNS

  Write the possessive form:

3.   a puppy belonging to three children

PARTS OF SPEECH: PRONOUNS

  Select the correct pronoun:

4.   Bill and _____ (I, me) are sure.

SENTENCE COMBINING:

5.   John's suitcase is packed.
     He is leaving for vacation tonight.

CAPITALIZATION:

1.   was virginia the first state in the united states of america?

PUNCTUATION:

   Punctuate these titles:

2.   A. (book)   Corduroy
      B. (story)   The Balloon

PARTS OF SPEECH: ADJECTIVES

   Select any adjective(s) telling <u>which ones</u>:

3.   Is this pencil darker than that pen?

SENTENCE TYPES:

   Give the sentence type:

4.   A.   The sofa is blue.
      B.   Will you help me?

SENTENCE COMBINING:

5.   The television is broken.
      David will repair it after school.

DAY 18

CAPITALIZATION:

1.   was cortes a spaniard* who conquered mexico?

       * a person from the country of Spain

PUNCTUATION:

   Punctuate these titles:

2.   A. (poem)   Holiday
     B. (story)   Tale of a Tail

PARTS OF SPEECH: ADJECTIVES

   Select any adjective(s) telling <u>what kind</u>:

3.   In the blue cool water swam a striped fish.

PARTS OF SPEECH: PRONOUNS

   Select the correct pronoun:

4.   May Barb and _____ (me, I) go to the library?

SENTENCE COMBINING:

5.   The children wore shorts.
     The children wore sandals.
     The children also wore tops.

CAPITALIZATION:
Capitalize these titles:

1. A. <u>the cat in the hat</u>
   B. "goldilocks and the three bears"

PUNCTUATION:

2. Bobs mother flew to St Augustine Florida

SENTENCE TYPES:
Determine the type of sentence:

3. A. Please come here.
   B. Has Jill arrived?

FRIENDLY LETTERS:
Determine the letter parts. Your choices are: greeting, closing, heading, signature, and message (body).

(A)   44 El m Street
Phoenix, Arizona 85013
April 1, 19--

(B) Dear Ryan,

(C) How are you? Do you have any idea when we will be attending the concert?

(D)   Your friend,
(E)   Collin

SENTENCE COMBINING:

5. A deer ate grass in the meadow.
   The meadow was wide and green.

DAY 20

CAPITALIZATION:

1.   the united bank building* is in downtown phoenix, arizona.

            * name of a particular building

PUNCTUATION:

2.   Hasnt Joel read Little Deer** to you

            ** title of a book

SENTENCE TYPES:

   Determine the type of sentence:

3.   A.   Will we run today?
       B.   We won!

PARTS OF SPEECH: VERBS

4.   A verb phrase is formed by adding a(an) _____verb
       to a main verb.

SENTENCE COMBINING:

5.   A teacher spoke about Indian life.
       The teacher is from Utah.

CAPITALIZATION:

1.   does steve sax still play for the los angeles dodgers*?

>   * name of a baseball team

PUNCTUATION:

2.   Yes Tammys dog had puppies

PARTS OF SPEECH: VERBS

Select the correct verb and underline the verb phrase twice.
Remember: verb phrase = helping verb + main verb

3.   The boy had _____ (ran, run) three miles.

PARTS OF SPEECH: NOUNS

Give the plural form:

4.   A.   holiday
      B.   study
      C.   dish
      D.   calf

SENTENCE COMBINING:

5.   The toddlers were playing with toy cars.
      The cars are yellow and red.

DAY 22

CAPITALIZATION:

1.   karen and i read <u>the tale of peter rabbit</u> by beatrix potter.

PUNCTUATION:

2.   Doesnt your uncle live in Orlando Florida

FRIENDLY LETTERS:

   Fill in the missing part of the heading of a letter:

3.   _____

                                                         _____

                                                         _____

       Dear Mrs. Cane,

PARTS OF SPEECH: ADJECTIVES

   Select any adjective(s) telling <u>which one</u>:

4.   These rods seem good, but I'll take that net.

SENTENCE COMBINING:

5.   The eagle perches on a limb.
      The limb is part of a dead tree.

CAPITALIZATION:

1.   is penn state university located in the nittany mountains?

PUNCTUATION:

2.   Cindy said Today is Tuesday

PARTS OF SPEECH: PRONOUNS

  Select the correct pronoun:

3.   This book was given to _____(I, me).

PARTS OF SPEECH: ADVERBS

  Select any adverb(s) telling how:

4.   She did her work fast but carefully.

SENTENCE COMBINING:

5.   A basket is hanging on her patio.
      The basket contains flowers.
      The flowers are bright yellow.

DAY 24

CAPITALIZATION:

1. a secretary at fann company ordered glass for the window.

PUNCTUATION:

2. Dear Vivian

   Hows the summer going for you

          A friend always
          Candy

PARTS OF SPEECH: ADVERBS

Select any adverb(s) telling <u>when</u>:

3. We planned to arrive early but arrived late.

SENTENCE TYPES:

Determine the type of sentence:

4.   A.   You're the winner!
      B.   Pass the butter.

SENTENCE COMBINING:

5. The trees were dropping their leaves.
   It was autumn.

CAPITALIZATION:

1.   on valentine's day we received a gift from chante chocolate store*.

          * name of a store

PUNCTUATION:

2.   Linda lets go swimming and play baseball

PARTS OF SPEECH: PRONOUNS

  Select the correct word:

3.   The dog wagged (it's , its) tail.

PARTS OF SPEECH: NOUNS

  Capitalize any proper noun:

4.   A.   friend   C.   iowa   E.   mountain
      B.   elizabeth   D.   november   F.   monday

SENTENCE COMBINING:

5.   Lily likes to ski.
      Lily likes to sled.
      Lily likes to ice skate.

DAY 26

CAPITALIZATION:

Capitalize the outline:

1.   i.   desert animals
          a.   rattlesnakes
          b.   turtles

PUNCTUATION:

2.   Our new address is 12 Link Drive Biglerville Pennsylvania   17307

SUBJECT / VERB:

Cross out prepositional phrases. Underline the subject once and the verb/verb phrase twice. Remember: verb phrase = helping verb + main verb:

3.   In the afternoon Grandma was reading in her room.

PARTS OF SPEECH: VERBS

Select the correct verb;   underline the verb phrase twice:

4.   We have _____(chose, chosen) a leader.

SENTENCE COMBINING:

5.   The rose was taken out of water.
       The rose wilted.
       The rose was red.

CAPITALIZATION:

1.   the students and mrs. blanch sang "america the beautiful."

PUNCTUATION:

2.   Was the Declaration of Independence signed July 4 1776

PARTS OF SPEECH: NOUNS

   Write the possessive form:

3.   a penny that belongs to Jimmy

PARTS OF SPEECH: ADVERBS

   Select any adverb(s) telling <u>where</u>:

4.   The children searched here and there but couldn't find it anywhere.

SENTENCE COMBINING:

5.   The butterfly is black and white.
      The butterfly is sitting on a tiny daisy.

DAY 28

CAPITALIZATION:

Capitalize these titles:

1. A. <u>monkey tales</u>
   B. "the brave knight"
   C. "hop to it"

PUNCTUATION:

Write the abbreviation:

2. A. Avenue   C. Mister   E. inch
   B. gallon   D. foot   F. Street

PARTS OF SPEECH: ADJECTIVES

Select any adjective(s) telling <u>how many</u>:

3. In the first class, there were thirty children.

PARTS OF SPEECH: VERBS

Select the correct verb; underline the verb phrase twice.
Remember: verb phrase = helping verb(s) + main verb:

4. Someone must have _____(went, gone) to the store.

SENTENCE COMBINING:

5. The water was cold.
   The water was for drinking.
   The water was in a glass.

CAPITALIZATION:

1.   carlos and his dog gumdrop went to an easter picnic.

PUNCTUATION:

   Write the correct abbreviation:

2.   A.   Doctor   C.   pound   E.   Drive
      B.   cup   D.   Company   F.   Lane

PARTS OF SPEECH: NOUNS

   Write the plural form:

3.   A.   ox
      B.   mouse
      C.   class
      D.   bus

SUBJECT / VERB:

   **Cross out prepositional phrases.   Underline the subject once
   and the verb/verb phrase twice.   Remember: verb phrase =
   helping verb(s) + main verb:**

4.   During the storm, the waves were rocking the boat at sea.

SENTENCE COMBINING:

5.   Todd rode his bike to Ted's house.
      Todd and Ted played chess.

DAY 30

CAPITALIZATION:

1.   have you read <u>little house on the prairie</u> at mesa library?

PUNCTUATION:

2.   Are we leaving at 1 15 P M today   asked Cheri

PARTS OF SPEECH: PRONOUNS

   Select the correct pronoun:

3.   John punched (I, me) playfully.

PARTS OF SPEECH: ADVERBS

   Select any adverb(s) telling <u>to what extent</u>:

4.   She was very tired but quite happy.

SENTENCE COMBINING:

5.   The toy was lying on the floor.
      Dad tripped over it.

CAPITALIZATION:

1.   last spring we visited niagara falls in new york.

PUNCTUATION:

2.   No the answer isnt twenty two

PARTS OF SPEECH: VERBS

   Select the correct verb; underline the verb phrase twice:

3.   The messenger should have _____ (gave, given) us the message.

PARTS OF SPEECH: NOUNS

   Write the possessive form:

4.   a book that belongs to Laura

SENTENCE COMBINING:

5.   The dentist examined Fay's teeth.
       Fay had no cavities.

DAY 32

CAPITALIZATION:

Capitalize these titles:

1.   A.   "jack and the beanstalk"
       B.   "all about america"
       C.   <u>gumdrop has a birthday</u>

PUNCTUATION:

2.   Yes her nephew lives in Tacoma Washington in the summer

PARTS OF SPEECH: VERBS

Select the correct verb; underline the verb phrase:

3.   The family had _____(drove, driven) many miles.

SUBJECT / VERB:

Cross out prepositional phrases; underline the subject once and the verb/verb phrase twice:

4.   The scuba diver arrived in a yellow car.

SENTENCE COMBINING:

5.   A kitten crawled on Tom's lap.
       The kitten was soft.
       The kitten was gray.

CAPITALIZATION:

1.   in a sears catalogue was a picture of a german clock.

PUNCTUATION:

Punctuate this heading:

2.   34 Lake Avenue
                                           Tucson Arizona   85705
                                           January 23 19--

PARTS OF SPEECH: ADVERBS

Select any adverb(s) telling <u>to what extent</u>:

3.   I'm so hungry, but I do not want chips.

PARTS OF SPEECH: PRONOUNS

Select the correct pronoun:

4.   The shopper and _____(she, her) went into a store.

SENTENCE COMBINING:

5.   The girls washed the car.
       The girls had fun.

DAY 34

CAPITALIZATION:
  Capitalize this poem:

1.   in a shoe box stuffed in an old nylon stocking
          sleeps the baby mouse I found in the meadow,
          where he trembled and shook beneath a stick
          till I caught him up by the tail and brought him in.

PUNCTUATION:

2.   Paula asked Is John ready

PARTS OF SPEECH: ADVERBS
  Select any adverb(s) that tell <u>how</u> or <u>when</u>:

3.   Suddenly, the ball was hit hard.

FRIENDLY LETTER: ENVELOPE
  Place your return address on this envelope:

4. _____

      _____

      _____

_____

SENTENCE COMBINING:

5.   Josh went to a movie.
          The movie was scary.
          The movie was about monsters.

CAPITALIZATION:

1.   did the japanese tourists take a boat down the ohio river?

PUNCTUATION:
Punctuate the heading, inside address, and greeting of a business letter:

2.

                                           2 Peat Street
                                         Plano Texas 75023
                                         October 21 19--

Gorm Industries
122 North 73rd Avenue
Tulsa Oklahoma 74145

Dear Sir

PARTS OF SPEECH: VERBS
Select the verb that agrees with the subject:

3.   This magazine (have, has) a page torn out.

PARTS OF SPEECH: PRONOUNS
Select the correct answer:

4.   (Me and Darin, Darin and I) are finished.

SENTENCE COMBINING:

5.   The fans cheered.
       They were watching a baseball game.

DAY 36

CAPITALIZATION:

1.   recently, dr. polk opened an office in the shea medical building.

PUNCTUATION:

2.   Randy may I read swim or hike today

SENTENCE TYPES:

  Determine the type of sentence:

3.   A.   The wall is white.
      B.   May I help you?

PARTS OF SPEECH: ADJECTIVES

  Select the correct adjective:

4.   Of the two sandpapers, this one is (rougher, roughest).

SENTENCE COMBINING:

5.   An ant crawled across the sidewalk.
      The ant was carrying a piece of bread.

CAPITALIZATION:

1.   a french poodle is for sale at the playful pet palace*.

       * name of store

PUNCTUATION:

2.   No we wont be there by 2 30 P M

PARTS OF SPEECH: ADJECTIVES

   Select the correct adjective:

3.   This picture is (more colorful,   most colorful) of the three.

SUBJECT / VERB:

   **Cross out prepositional phrases. Underline the subject once and
   the verb/verb phrase twice. Remember: verb phrase = helping verb(s)
   + main verb:**

4.   Some of the sheep were moved to a new field.

SENTENCE COMBINING:

5.   A carnival will be held soon.
       A carnival will be held to raise money for the fire department.

DAY 38

CAPITALIZATION:

1.   a chinese student will stay with the birk family in august.

PUNCTUATION:

2.   Will you be in Topeka Kansas next week Marvin

PARTS OF SPEECH: NOUNS

Capitalize proper nouns:

3.   A.   gulf of mexico   C.   lake   E.   mississippi river
      B.   river   D.   lake erie   F.   street

PARTS OF SPEECH: ADVERBS

Select the correct word:

4.   That chef bakes very (good, well).

SENTENCE COMBINING:

5.   The boys ran a race.
      Dave won.

CAPITALIZATION:

1.   have you seen the statue of liberty in new york city?

PUNCTUATION:

2.   Jerry exclaimed Jump on

PARTS OF SPEECH: VERBS

Write the contraction:

3.   A.   do not   C.   they are   E.   I have
      B.   I will   D.   has not   F.   she will

SENTENCE TYPES:

Determine the type of sentence:

4.   A.   Is the circus coming?
      B.   Go away.

SENTENCE COMBINING:

5.   The small child cried.
      The small child had an ear infection.

DAY 40

CAPITALIZATION:

1.   one ruler of england was queen victoria.

PUNCTUATION:

   Punctuate this outline:

2.   I   Famous airplanes
             A   <u>Spirit of St. Louis</u>
             B   <u>Spruce Goose</u>
      II   Famous ships

PARTS OF SPEECH: ADVERBS

   Select any adverb(s) telling <u>when</u> or <u>where</u>:

3.   Never go outside without permission.

PARTS OF SPEECH:

   Select the correct word:

4.   Your report is (to, too, two) short.

SENTENCE COMBINING:

5.   Lois read a book.
      The book contained one hundred pages.

CAPITALIZATION:

1.   did reverend sells preach at st. james lutheran church?

PUNCTUATION:

2.   Millie asked When is the party

PARTS OF SPEECH: VERBS

 Select the main verb:

3.   Joan has gone to the mall.

PARTS OF SPEECH: NOUNS

 Write the plural form:

4.   A.   pen
      B.   wish
      C.   monkey
      D.   deer
      E.   envelope

SENTENCE COMBINING:

5.   The puppy is in the backyard.
      The puppy is chasing a ball.

DAY 42

CAPITALIZATION:

1.   when a. t. arkin left chicago's airport, it was snowing.

PUNCTUATION:

2.   Joyce laughed loudly but her sister cried

PARTS OF SPEECH: NOUNS

   Write the plural form:

3.   A.   flash
        B.   story
        C.   child
        D.   bay
        E.   film

SENTENCE TYPES:

   Determine the type of sentence:

4.   A.   Give me that, please.
        B.   They're here!
        C.   This costs a dime.

SENTENCE COMBINING:

5.   The child sneezed.
        The child coughed.
        The child took a tissue from the box.

CAPITALIZATION:

1.   the poem "the midnight ride of paul revere" begins, "listen, my children..."

PUNCTUATION:

Punctuate this outline:

2.   I   Parts of speech
             A   Nouns
             B   Pronouns
       II   Word parts
             A   Prefixes
             B   Suffixes

PARTS OF SPEECH:

Select the correct word:

3.   (Their, They're, There) teacher is absent.

PARTS OF SPEECH: NOUNS

Write the possessive form:

4.   a house belonging to Tom and Nancy

SENTENCE COMBINING:

5.   The car is painted red.
        The car has a flat tire.

DAY 44

CAPITALIZATION:

1.   a meeting of the gleeful gardeners' club* was held at ingle inn.

            * name of a club

PUNCTUATION:

2.   Who is your leader asked Carl

PARTS OF SPEECH: ADVERBS

   Select any adverb(s) telling <u>when</u>:

3.   Do you want to dance now or later?

PARTS OF SPEECH: ADJECTIVES

   Select any adjective(s) that tell <u>how many</u>:

4.   A few boys brought only one friend to the game.

SENTENCE COMBINING:

5.   Mary writes letters.
      Mary writes to her aunt.
      Mary also writes letters to her cousin.

CAPITALIZATION:

1.   dear mr. flan,

          your poem entitled "from a funny bear" is good.

                              sincerely yours,
                              meg lewis

PUNCTUATION:

2.   I like the ice cream   said the clown

PARTS OF SPEECH: ADJECTIVES

  Select any adjective(s) that tell <u>how many</u>:

3.   Some flowers were blooming in their two gardens.

SUBJECT / VERB:

  **Underline the subject once and the verb/verb phrase twice.
  Remember: verb phrase = helping verb(s) + main verb:**

4.   A storm had blown trees down.

SENTENCE COMBINING:

5.   The candy bar was left in the sun.
      The candy bar melted.

DAY 46

CAPITALIZATION:

1.   two chinese tourists went with us to the empire state building*.

* name of a particular building

PUNCTUATION:

2.   They ate pizza drank cola and played ball

PARTS OF SPEECH: NOUNS

Write the possessive form:

3.   a lamb belonging to two girls

PARTS OF SPEECH: VERBS

Select the correct verb:

4.   Aunt Joan often (come, comes) for a few hours.

SENTENCE COMBINING:

5.   Tracey's sneakers were under the bed.
Tracey couldn't find them.

CAPITALIZATION:

1. has c. t. smith ever been to yosemite national park in the spring?

PUNCTUATION:

2. The R J Lincoln Co opened last Thursday Nov 29

SUBJECT / VERB:

Underline the subject once and the verb/verb phrase twice:

3. Dave and I will fish tomorrow.

SENTENCE TYPES:

Determine the type of sentence:

4. A. Go this way.
    B. Look out!
    C. Have you finished?

SENTENCE COMBINING:

5. My uncle teaches art.
    My uncle teaches at a junior high.
    My uncle's name is Phil.

DAY 48

CAPITALIZATION:

1. many americans fly flags on veterans' day.

PUNCTUATION:

2. Id like to see that play   Sharon said

PARTS OF SPEECH: NOUNS

 Write the possessive form:

3. books belonging to a librarian

PARTS OF SPEECH: ADVERBS

 Select any adverb(s) telling <u>how</u>:

4. He quietly gave the answer.

SENTENCE   COMBINING:

5. A play began today.
    The play is being performed at Dikson School.

CAPITALIZATION:

1.   their friends went to glenrok art museum last friday.

PUNCTUATION:

2.   His brother was born on Feb 6 1984 in a local hospital

PARTS OF SPEECH: ADJECTIVES

  Select any adjective(s) telling <u>which one</u>:

3.   These shoes should match that dress.

PARTS OF SPEECH: ADVERBS

  Select the correct form:

4.   Susan runs (faster, more fast) than Joe.

SENTENCE COMBINING:

5.   Rob threw the ball.
       Sally caught the ball.

DAY 50

CAPITALIZATION:

1.   will he read "the story of old king cole" soon?

PUNCTUATION:

   Punctuate these titles:

2.   A.   (book)   Moby Dick
      B.   (story)   Millie
      C.   (poem)   If
      D.   (magazine)   Teen

PARTS OF SPEECH: VERBS

   Select the verb that agrees with the subject:

3.   The winners (doesn't, don't) get a trophy.

PARTS OF SPEECH: NOUNS

   Write the plural form:

4.   A.   box
      B.   brush
      C.   ray
      D.   mouse
      E.   secretary

SENTENCE COMBINING:

5.   Susan collects stickers.
      Susan collects stamps.
      Susan also collects shells.

CAPITALIZATION:

1. is the statue of liberty in new york city located on liberty island?

PUNCTUATION:

2. Amys report isnt finished yet

FRIENDLY LETTERS:

Select the correct closing:

3. A.   Truly Yours,
    B.   Truly yours,

PARTS OF SPEECH: PRONOUNS

Select the correct pronoun:

4. Mother nudged _____ (me, I) and smiled.

SENTENCE COMBINING:

5. Sally's lock was broken.
    Sally bought a new one.

DAY 52

CAPITALIZATION:

1.   little jonathon has read the book <u>the sesame street treasury</u>.

PUNCTUATION:

2.   Wow Ive jumped nearly four feet Mrs Dill

PARTS OF SPEECH: NOUNS

  Determine if the noun is common or proper:

3.   A.   Jane
      B.   glue
      C.   canary
      D.   Thorn Theater
      E.   school

PARTS OF SPEECH: VERBS

  Select the verb that agrees with the subject:

4.   Our telephone (rings, ring) often.

SENTENCE COMBINING:

5.   We watched television.
      We ate popcorn.

CAPITALIZATION:

1. last summer mrs. kirk's class went to the library on elton street.

PUNCTUATION:

2. Junes pen wont work on this three ply paper

PARTS OF SPEECH: PRONOUNS

Select the correct possessive pronoun:

3. The birds left (its, their) nest for food.

SUBJECT / VERB:

Cross out prepositional phrases. Underline the subject once and The verb/verb phrase twice:

4. At dawn some swans swam on a pond.

SENTENCE COMBINING:

5. The man drew a picture.
    The man is an artist.
    The picture was of a clown.

DAY 54

CAPITALIZATION:

1.   333 strom street
                                                                         shippensburg, pa   17257
                                                                         april 22, 19--

        dear larry,

PUNCTUATION:

2.   Bobbi said Yes I am ready

SUBJECT / VERB:

   **Cross out prepositional phrases. Underline the subject once and
   the verb/verb phrase twice:**

3.   A white furry bunny hopped into our garden.

PARTS OF SPEECH: NOUNS

   Capitalize any proper noun:

4.   A.   xerox corporation
          B.   mummy mountain
          C.   newspaper
          D.   fido
          E.   springer spaniel   (breed of dog)

SENTENCE COMBINING:

5.   The dessert is delicious.
          The dessert is pie.
          The pie is apple.

CAPITALIZATION:

1.   have i received my copy of <u>your big backyard</u> * ?

              * title of a magazine

PUNCTUATION:

2.   Dad wheres Sen Blatz going

PARTS OF SPEECH: NOUNS

  Write the possessive form:

3.   a candy bar belonging to some girls

PARTS OF SPEECH: PREPOSITIONS

  Identify any prepositional phrase(s):

4.   The rug in the middle of the room is from China.

SENTENCE COMBINING:

5.   The test was difficult.
      The test was about fractions.

DAY 56

CAPITALIZATION:

1. in july, the south mountain fair is held.

PUNCTUATION:

2. The story entitled Pinocchio isnt sad

PARTS OF SPEECH: ADVERBS

Select any adverb(s) telling <u>how</u>:

3. Eagerly, she hit the golf ball hard.

PARTS OF SPEECH: ADJECTIVES

4. The three articles that will always be adjectives are _____, _____, and _____.

SENTENCE COMBINING:

5. Jill went ice skating.
   Jill's brother went sledding.

CAPITALIZATION:

1.   the r. o. dott co. is located on east elm lane in lubbock, texas.

PUNCTUATION:

2.   I want a sandwich remarked Brett

PARTS OF SPEECH: ADJECTIVES

   Select the correct adjective:

3.   (Those, Them) glasses are mine.

PARTS OF SPEECH: ADVERBS

   Select any adverb(s) telling <u>when</u>:

4.   Now and then, we stop for a rest.

SENTENCE COMBINING:

5.   The owl sat in a tree.
       The owl hooted.

DAY 58

CAPITALIZATION:

1.   the title of his report is "taking care of your pet."

PUNCTUATION:

2.   Mr Jones thinks that the childrens playground needs grass

PARTS OF SPEECH: ADVERBS

   Select any adverb(s) telling <u>where</u>:

3.   The teacher looked up and wrote something down.

FRIENDLY LETTERS: ENVELOPE

   Write your return address on this envelope:

4.
_____
_____
_____

_____

SENTENCE COMBINING:

5.   Gloria was shouting for her brother.
      Gloria became hoarse.

CAPITALIZATION:

1.   when sam left the united states marine corps, he returned to college.

PUNCTUATION:

2.   Theyre arriving late and Ill pick them up at the airport

PARTS OF SPEECH: ADJECTIVES

Select the correct adjective:

3.   That building is (taller, tallest) than this one.

PARTS OF SPEECH: CONJUNCTIONS

4.   The three coordinating conjunctions are _____, _____, and _____.

SENTENCE COMBINING:

5.   The message was sent in a letter.
     The message was written in ink.
     The message was written by Alice.

DAY 60

CAPITALIZATION:

1.   have mr. lott and dr. jones played tennis at the top seed club?

PUNCTUATION:

2.   Toms uncle was born Jan 30 1950 in Ohio

PARTS OF SPEECH: ADVERBS

   Select any adverb(s) telling <u>when</u>:

3.   Tomorrow, we shall leave early for church.

SUBJECT / VERB:

   Cross out prepositional phrases. Underline the subject once and the verb/verb phrase twice. Remember: verb phrase = helping verb(s) + main verb:

4.   In the morning, Mom and Dad are driving to Montana.

SENTENCE COMBINING:

5.   The road is dirt.
      The road has many loose stones.
      The road is bumpy.

CAPITALIZATION:

1.　the inventor of the phonograph was thomas a. edison.

PUNCTUATION:

2.　George have you been to St Louis Missouri in the winter

PARTS OF SPEECH:　VERBS

Write the contraction:

3.　A.　have not
　　B.　you are
　　C.　he will
　　D.　they have
　　E.　I am

PARTS OF SPEECH:　ADJECTIVES

Select any adjective telling <u>how many</u>:

4.　Their two friends gave them some candy.

SENTENCE COMBINING:

5.　The concert was cancelled.
　　The singer was sick.

DAY 62

CAPITALIZATION:

1.   their alaskan guests stayed at the blue moose lodge.

PUNCTUATION:

2.   Carrie exclaimed Look at that boat

PARTS OF SPEECH: NOUNS

   Write the plural form:

3.   A.   boy
      B.   crash
      C.   buzz
      D.   field
      E.   baby

SENTENCE TYPES:

   Determine the type of sentence:

4.   A.   Will you join this club?
      B.   The rain has stopped.
      C.   Take this to your sister.

SENTENCE COMBINING:

5.   Mom made sandwiches.
      Dad made a salad.
      The food was for lunch.

DAY 63

CAPITALIZATION:

1.　my friend and i took white cliff road to the game.

PUNCTUATION:

2.　Lori stand up and Ill measure you

PARTS OF SPEECH: PRONOUNS

　Select the correct pronoun:

3.　Jill and _____ (I,　me) were selected.

PARTS OF SPEECH: ADJECTIVES

　Select any adjective(s) telling <u>what kind</u>:

4.　Lynn's blue shirt matches your red skirt.

SENTENCE COMBINING:

5.　Juice was served first.
　　It was orange juice.
　　Milk was served later.

DAY 64

CAPITALIZATION:

1.   the swartz family visited dade county in florida.

PUNCTUATION:

2.   52 Elm Ln
                                                                         Gettysburg PA   17325
                                                                         May 8 19--

     Dear Sam

PARTS OF SPEECH: VERBS

   Select the correct verb;   underline the verb phrase:

3.   We had _____ (eaten, ate) at noon.

PARTS OF SPEECH: NOUNS

   Write the possessive form:

4.   a fork belonging to Chris

SENTENCE COMBINING:

5.   Rudy runs fast.
        Nancy runs faster.

CAPITALIZATION:

1.   was yankee stadium in new york built recently?

PUNCTUATION:

2.   Wow We did it Sean

PARTS OF SPEECH: PRONOUNS

   Select any pronoun(s):

3.   They left their money at home.

PARTS OF SPEECH: VERBS

   Write the contraction:

4.   A.   could not
      B.   it is
      C.   I am
      D.   cannot
      E.   will not

SENTENCE COMBINING:

5.   Randy had a party.
      It was a birthday party.
      Fifteen friends attended.

DAY 66

CAPITALIZATION:

1.   a chinese restaurant called ming's golden dragon opened thursday.

PUNCTUATION:

2.   Is Rebeccas horse Mr Pratt ready to ride

PARTS OF SPEECH: VERBS

3.   List the 23 helping (auxiliary) verbs.

PARTS OF SPEECH:
      Select the correct word:

4.   (Their, There, They're) uncle is a carpenter.

SENTENCE COMBINING:

5.   The day was cold.
      The day was windy.
      The day was sunny.

CAPITALIZATION:

1.   did you know that the fourth of july is called independence day?

PUNCTUATION:

2.   One third of Marges doll collection is from London England

PARTS OF SPEECH: PRONOUNS

   Select the correct pronoun:

3.   (We, Us) boys must meet.

PARTS OF SPEECH: ADVERBS

   Select any adverb(s) telling how:

4.   The salesman wrote slowly and carefully.

SENTENCE COMBINING:

5.   The floor is wet.
      Cameron has spilled lemonade.

DAY 68

CAPITALIZATION:

1.   at dobson theater the group saw <u>the king and i</u>.

PUNCTUATION:

 Use underlining or quotation marks:

2.   A.   (book)   Tex
     B.   (story)   Cat and the Underworld
     C.   (magazine)   Ranger Rick

PARTS OF SPEECH: VERBS

 Select the verb that agrees with the subject:

3.   The clown also (sing, sings) in his act.

SENTENCE TYPES:

 Determine the type of sentence:

4.   A.   That's more like it!
     B.   Take this paper, please.
     C.   Jimmy is here.

SENTENCE COMBINING:

5.   Her hair is brown.
     Her hair is curly.
     Her hair needs to be combed.

CAPITALIZATION:

1. his birthday is in february on presidents' day.

PUNCTUATION:

2. Moms exercise class will meet Friday at 2 P M

FRIENDLY LETTER:

Label the parts of this friendly letter:

3.
                       (A)   22 Doe Lane
                                   Ogden, Utah
                                   May 9, 19--

Dear Sonya,   (B)

   We are having a great time here. We will be home soon.   (C)

                              Love,   (D)
                              Chris   (E)

PARTS OF SPEECH: VERBS

4. A verb phrase always has _____.

SENTENCE COMBINING:

5. The fair will be held next week.
It is a state fair.
We are going.

DAY 70

CAPITALIZATION:

1.   on monday, mayor tilson flew on american airlines to salem, oregon.

PUNCTUATION:

2.   Im wondering if youve read Blubber *

         * book title

PARTS OF SPEECH: VERBS

3.   List the 23 helping (auxiliary) verbs.

PARTS OF SPEECH: ADVERBS

  Select the correct word to avoid using double negatives:

4.   He doesn't remember (nothing, anything) about the incident.

SENTENCE COMBINING:

5.   Mrs. Patts is a pilot.
     Mrs. Patts owns an airplane.

CAPITALIZATION:

1.   has senator r. c. cline been re-elected to congress?

PUNCTUATION:

2.   Sally asked   Wheres Mikes new boat

PARTS OF SPEECH: VERBS

  Select the correct verb;   underline the verb phrase twice:

3.   I should have (known, knew) the answer.

PARTS OF SPEECH: PRONOUNS

  Select the correct pronoun:

4.   Jake told (he, him) the joke.

SENTENCE COMBINING:

5.   The boys were watching television.
      The boys were lying on the floor.
      The boys were eating popcorn.

DAY 72

CAPITALIZATION:

1. when aunt bea came, she arrived on the <u>elton golden express</u>.

PUNCTUATION:

2. No I wont go and Tami doesnt want to go either

PARTS OF SPEECH: ADVERBS

   Select any adverb(s) telling <u>to what extent</u>:

3. In a rather old barn lives a very odd mouse.

PARTS OF SPEECH: VERBS

   Select the correct verb:

4. Please (set, sit) down.

SENTENCE COMBINING:

5. The lake is very deep.
    The lake is called Crater Lake.
    The lake is in Oregon.

CAPITALIZATION:

1.   did dad stay at the anaheim hilton hotel across from disneyland?

PUNCTUATION:

2.   Joy asked Have you read The Staircase*

   * book title

PARTS OF SPEECH: PRONOUNS

   Select the correct pronoun:

3.   May Bill and _____ (I, me) go to the library?

PARTS OF SPEECH:

   Select the correct word:

4.   Have you seen (them, those) kittens?

SENTENCE COMBINING:

5.   That shop sells flowers.
   That shop opened last week.
   I bought some daisies.

DAY 74

CAPITALIZATION:

1.   on veterans' day, a parade marched down culver avenue to loe park.

PUNCTUATION:

2.   The mens club listened to a speech entitled Time Wasters

PARTS OF SPEECH: CONJUNCTIONS

3.   The three coordinating conjunctions are _____, _____, and _____.

SUBJECT / VERB:

  Cross out prepositional phrase(s). Underline the subject once and the verb/verb phrase twice. Remember: verb phrase = helping verb(s) + main verb:

4.   Many of the flowers had already bloomed.

SENTENCE COMBINING:

5.   The vase was a ceramic one.
       The vase was pink.
       The vase was filled with straw.

CAPITALIZATION:

1.   for lunch we ate canadian bacon sandwiches at max's deli*.

      *restaurant name

PUNCTUATION:

2.   Kim said My brother is twenty one years old

PARTS OF SPEECH: NOUNS

   Determine if the noun is common or proper:

3.   A.   steak
      B   Hildale Bank
      C.   Redfield Road
      D.   Yankee Stadium
      E.   shepherd

PARTS OF SPEECH: ADJECTIVES

   Select adjective(s) telling <u>how many</u>:

4.   A few joggers ran six miles today.

SENTENCE COMBINING:

5.   Joanie went ice skating.
      Her sister went, too.
      They went to Bardton Pond.

DAY 76

CAPITALIZATION:

1.   last spring she went to china to study the buddhistic religion.

PUNCTUATION:

2.   The boys restroom and the locker room wont be open

PARTS OF SPEECH: ADVERBS

  Select the correct adverb form:

3.   This work was done (more carefully, most carefully) than yours.

PARTS OF SPEECH: ADJECTIVES

4.   The three articles that are always adjectives are _____, _____, and _____.

SENTENCE COMBINING:

5.   Jim's lunch is in the refrigerator.
       The lunch consists of a sandwich and cookies.

CAPITALIZATION:

1.   a swiss airliner landed at kennedy airport in new york.

PUNCTUATION:

2.   At 10 00 A M on Saturday May 12 1965 the couple met

PARTS OF SPEECH: VERBS

   Select the correct verb;   underline the verb phrase twice:

3.   Has the biker _____ (rode, ridden) two miles?

SENTENCE TYPES:

   Determine the type of sentence:

4.   A.   Are you going?
        B.   Mary asked if we were going.
        C.   Please go.

SENTENCE COMBINING:

5.   This watch is new.
        This watch is blue.
        This watch was given to Barbara as a graduation gift.

DAY 78

CAPITALIZATION:

1.   our governor will meet with mayor dobbs at terrace guest house.

PUNCTUATION:

2.   Joe read Where the Red Fern Grows* and he wrote a report

          * book title

SUBJECT / VERB:

Cross out prepositional phrase(s). Underline the subject once and the verb/verb phrase twice:

3.   Marta, Tina, and Bob will be rehearsing in an hour.

PARTS OF SPEECH: ADVERBS

4.   The seven adverbs that tell **to what extent** are _____, _____, _____, _____, _____, _____, and _____.

SENTENCE COMBINING:

5.   They went fishing at a lake.
       They caught five fish.
       Mom and Dad went.

CAPITALIZATION:

1. during labor day weekend, rev. little's family went to the zoo.

PUNCTUATION:

2. Mark asked Wheres the three pronged fork

PARTS OF SPEECH: ADJECTIVES

Select any adjective(s) telling <u>how many</u>:

3. Some palm trees were planted in seven large planters.

PARTS OF SPEECH: NOUNS

Write the plural form:

4. A. moose
   B. friend
   C. gulf
   D. fence
   E. church

SENTENCE COMBINING:

5. The bike race began.
   I fell off my bike.
   I skinned my knee.

DAY 80

CAPITALIZATION:

1.   did uncle bill read the <u>hotel herald</u>* at the los angeles convention center?

          * magazine title

PUNCTUATION:

2.   The librarian read to us gave us a quiz and graded the papers

PARTS OF SPEECH: PREPOSITIONS

   Select object(s) of the preposition:

3.   Throughout the day rain pounded on the roof.

FRIENDLY LETTER:

4.   Compose a heading.

SENTENCE COMBINING:

5.   Two girls played dominoes.
        Three boys read books.
        The teacher had given us free time.

CAPITALIZATION:

1. the announcer said, "we are pleased to have professor gibb here."

PUNCTUATION:

Punctuate these titles:

2. A. (song) Arise and Shine
B. (book) Roll of Thunder, Hear My Cry
C. (chapter) Verbs
D. (poem) On a Rainy Day

PARTS OF SPEECH: ADJECTIVES

3. The four demonstrative adjectives are _____, _____, _____, and _____.

PARTS OF SPEECH: NOUNS

Write the plural form:

4. A. pie
B. flash
C. derby
D. pay
E. ox

SENTENCE COMBINING:

5. His shoes are blue.
His shoes are tennis shoes.
His shoes are in the corner of the room.

DAY 82

CAPITALIZATION:

1.   the german ambassador visited san francisco during the korean war.

PUNCTUATION:

2.   Paul wont you take this self propelling object to the park

PARTS OF SPEECH: NOUNS

  Write the possessive form:

3.   a business belonging to five ladies

SUBJECT / VERB:

  Cross out prepositional phrase(s). Underline the subject once and the verb/verb phrase twice:

4.   Martha's uncle and her cousin will be in that race.

SENTENCE COMBINING:

5.   Tom's aunt is a teacher.
      Her name is Susan Bothe.

CAPITALIZATION:

1.   the arbor day* celebration included a tree planting at fimm park.

        * name of a special day

PUNCTUATION:

2.   Sue asked   Hows your grandmother feeling Julie

PARTS OF SPEECH: VERBS

  Write the tense of the verb:

3.   A.   Mary **walks** to the market.
       B.   Cal **walked** his dog.

FRIENDLY LETTER:

4.   Write the closing and signature of a friendly letter:

SENTENCE COMBINING:

5.   That horse is a palomino.
       That horse is named Colonel.

DAY 84

CAPITALIZATION:

1.   has the liberty bell always been at independence hall?

PUNCTUATION:

2.   Sallys flight leaves on Friday June 8th at 12 30 A M

PARTS OF SPEECH: NOUNS

  Write the possessive form:

3.   a flag belonging to Ted and Jay

PARTS OF SPEECH: PRONOUNS

  Select the correct pronoun:

4.   Did Dick and (her, she) do the project together?

SENTENCE COMBINING:

5.   The wagon has black tires.
      The wagon is painted green.
      The wagon has a new handle.

CAPITALIZATION:

1.   "this is a special meal," said ruth.

PUNCTUATION:

2.   Sarahs first teacher was Miss Dow

PARTS OF SPEECH: VERBS

3.   Write the forms of the verb infinitive <u>to be</u>.

PARTS OF SPEECH: PRONOUNS

  Select the correct pronoun:

4.   The cat licked (it's, its) paws.

SENTENCE COMBINING:

5.   It rained all day.
      The children had to stay inside.

DAY 86

CAPITALIZATION:

1. on mothers' day, we took mom to a mexican food restaurant.

PUNCTUATION:

2. Dont go pleaded Peter

PARTS OF SPEECH: ADJECTIVES

3. The three articles that are always adjectives are _____, _____, and _____.

PARTS OF SPEECH: NOUNS

   Give the possessive form:

4. pancakes that belong to Sue and James

SENTENCE COMBINING:

5. A monkey was sitting on a tree limb.
    Another monkey was swinging on a rope.

CAPITALIZATION:

Capitalize these titles:

1.   A.   "a bicycle built for two"
       B.   <u>days of our lives</u>
       C.   <u>the night before christmas</u>
       D.   <u>to sir, with love</u>

PUNCTUATION:

2.   Jans sister in law is from Toledo Ohio

PARTS OF SPEECH: ADVERBS

Select the correct adverb form:

3.   Of the three contestants, he hit the ball (hardest, harder).

PARTS OF SPEECH: NOUNS

Determine if the noun is abstract or concrete:

4.   A.   desk
       B.   love
       C.   honesty
       D.   building

SENTENCE COMBINING:

5.   An invitation to a wedding came in the mail.
       Gail and Gabe will be marrying.

DAY 88

CAPITALIZATION:

1. when bill and i go to bree mall, we shop at chris's craft cabin*.

    * store name

PUNCTUATION:

2. Lyle asked Isnt your dad coming at 3 30 P M for you

PARTS OF SPEECH: NOUNS

Write the possessive form:

3. a ball belonging to two babies

SENTENCE TYPES:

Determine the type of sentence:

4. A. The phone is ringing.
    B. Are you sure?
    C. We're ready!
    D. Please stay here.

SENTENCE COMBINING:

5. Jill gave the clerk a dollar.
    Jill bought a candy bar.
    The clerk gave Jill the change.

CAPITALIZATION:

1.   a memorial day parade honored those who had fought in world war II.

PUNCTUATION:

2.   In Readers Digest there is an article entitled Young America

PARTS OF SPEECH: PRONOUNS

  Select the correct pronoun:

3.   George wants (those, them) shoes.

PARTS OF SPEECH: NOUNS

  Write the possessive form:

4.   some bugs belonging to some children

SENTENCE COMBINING:

5.   Jean read an article in the newspaper.
      The article said that a circus would be coming to town.

DAY 90

CAPITALIZATION:

1.   in november the members of the u. s. house of representatives met.

PUNCTUATION:

2.   Cindys essay entitled Americas Story isnt finished

PARTS OF SPEECH: PREPOSITIONS

  Select the object(s) of the preposition:

3.   On Friday and Saturday, a yard sale was held.

PARTS OF SPEECH: ADJECTIVES

  Select any demonstrative adjective(s):

4.   This award was presented to that student.

SENTENCE   COMBINING:

5.   The sky was black.
      It looked like a storm was coming.

CAPITALIZATION:

1.   the shoshone indian tribe must be proud of sacajawea*.

         * famous female guide

PUNCTUATION:

2.   Teri havent you found a book a pen or a notebook

PARTS OF SPEECH: PRONOUNS

  Select the correct pronoun:

3.   The girl left _____ (their, her) lunch in the cafeteria.

PARTS OF SPEECH: VERBS

  Cross out prepositional phrase(s). Underline the subject once and the verb/verb phrase twice. Remember: verb phrase = helping verb(s) + main verb:

4.   The director and her crew had filmed the movie at night.

SENTENCE COMBINING:

5.   The necklace was made of noodles.
       Cody made it in nursery school.

DAY 92

CAPITALIZATION:

1.   we ate swedish meat balls at elegante cafe* on elm street.

          * name of restaurant

PUNCTUATION:

   Punctuate these titles:

2.   A.   (magazine) Insights
      B.   (poem)   If
      C.   (newspaper) Chicago Tribune
      D.   (song)   Katie

PARTS OF SPEECH: VERBS

   Write the present and past tense:

3.   A.   **to give:**
              1.   Present: Today I _____or he/she _____.
              2.   Past: Yesterday Linn _____.

      B.   **to walk:**
              1.   Present: Today I _____or he/she _____.
              2.   Past: Yesterday Linn _____.

PARTS OF SPEECH: ADVERBS

   Select any adverb(s) telling <u>where:</u>

4.   The bird watcher looked up and knew where the robin was.

SENTENCE COMBINING:

5.   We went to the zoo.
      We saw a mother gorilla.
      We also saw her baby.

CAPITALIZATION:

1.   for our thanksgiving feast, mississippi mud pie was served.

PUNCTUATION:

2.   Marty wheres the TV Guide

PARTS OF SPEECH: NOUNS

  Write the plural form:

3.   A.   face
        B.   story
        C.   wish
        D.   piano
        E.   goose

PARTS OF SPEECH: VERBS

  Write the past tense of the infinitive:

4.   A.   **to sing**
        B.   **to yell**

SENTENCE   COMBINING:

5.   The check is on the table.
        The check is for your lunch.

DAY 94

CAPITALIZATION:

1.   every christmas eve the gray family attends a baptist church service.

PUNCTUATION:

2.   The Rev R Dobbs spoke about life in 1215 B C

PARTS OF SPEECH:

3.   What part of speech is **Wow!**?

PARTS OF SPEECH: VERBS

  Write the past participle form:

4.   A.   **to give:**   has/have/had _____

       B.   **to walk:**   has/have/had_____

SENTENCE COMBINING:

5.   The glue stick was on the floor.
       Jim picked it up.

CAPITALIZATION:

1.   did mayor link sail on a french liner in the atlantic ocean?

PUNCTUATION:

   Punctuate this outline:

2.   I   Important holidays
              A   Memorial Day
              B   Armistice Day

      II   Special Days
              A   April Fools' Day
              B   Ground Hog's Day

PARTS OF SPEECH: ADVERBS

3.   The seven adverbs that tell **to what extent** are _____, _____,
      _____, _____, _____, _____, and _____.

SUBJECT / VERB:

   **Cross out prepositional phrase(s). Underline the subject
   once and the verb/verb phrase twice:**

4.   At our picnic in the spring, Jenny and her dad played ball.

SENTENCE COMBINING:

5.   Milly and Cal are riding horses.
      They went for a ride in the forest.

DAY 96

CAPITALIZATION:

1. has william perry ever played for the chicago bears* ?

   * name of a football team

PUNCTUATION:

2. Ted two thirds of the peaches wont be sold

PARTS OF SPEECH: ADJECTIVES

  Select the articles:

3. On the table lay a banana and an orange.

PARTS OF SPEECH: PRONOUNS

  Select the correct pronoun:

4. May Ryan and _____ (I , me) take that?

SENTENCE COMBINING:

5. Micah planted six tomato plants.
   The plants grew large.
   The plants produced many tomatoes.

CAPITALIZATION:

1.   next july our club will visit the dallas museum of art in texas.

PUNCTUATION:

2.   This week we expect twenty one inches of snow said the lady

PARTS OF SPEECH: VERBS

   Select the correct verb; underline the verb phrase twice:

3.   The diver must have _____ (broke, broken) a record.

PARTS OF SPEECH: ADJECTIVES

   Select any adjective(s) telling <u>how many:</u>

4.   One artist had many paintings in the display.

SENTENCE COMBINING:

5.   The stapler was empty.
      Sheri filled it.

DAY 98

CAPITALIZATION:

1. in the autumn, senator lee will go to columbia, south america.

PUNCTUATION:

Punctuate this friendly letter:

2.
                                              2 Doe Street   (A)
                                              Scottsdale Arizona 85254
                                              March 7   19--

    Dear Tom   (B)

        How are you doing   Well see you in a few months   (C)

                                              Your friend   (D)
                                              Matt   (E)

FRIENDLY LETTER:

3. The parts of a friendly letter are (A)_____, (B)_____,
    (C)_____, (D)_____, and (E)_____.

PARTS OF SPEECH: VERBS

4. List the 23 helping (auxiliary) verbs.

SENTENCE COMBINING:

5. The cake is in the oven.
    The cake is for Joe's birthday.
    The cake is chocolate.

CAPITALIZATION:

1.   h. b. hicks company sells indian jewelry in ohio.

PUNCTUATION:

2.   At 9 00 P M on Friday July 4th there will be fireworks

SUBJECT / VERB:

Cross out prepositional phrase(s). Underline the subject once and the verb/verb phrase twice:

3.   Some of the dogs stayed near their masters during the show.

PARTS OF SPEECH: NOUNS

Determine if the noun is concrete or abstract:

4.   A.   truth
        B.   friendship
        C.   chairs
        D.   sky
        E.   love

SENTENCE COMBINING:

5.   His mother put drops in his ear.
        He has an ear infection.
        His name is Richard.

DAY 100

CAPITALIZATION:

1.　his daughter studies american literature at the university of iowa.

PUNCTUATION:

2.　Your report Lisa is due Friday Sept 8 at noon

PARTS OF SPEECH:　VERBS

Write the contraction:

3.	A.	they have	E.	she has
	B.	does not	F.	is not
	C.	I will	G.	cannot
	D.	will not	H.	she would

PARTS OF SPEECH:　PRONOUNS

Select the correct pronoun:

4.　This letter is for you and _____ (I, me) .

SENTENCE COMBINING:

5.　The children bought their dad a gift.
　　The gift was for Fathers' Day.
　　The gift was a book.

CAPITALIZATION:

1.   in our reading class, we read "the legend of sleepy hollow."

PUNCTUATION:

2.   Youre the greatest said the coach so try your best

PARTS OF SPEECH: VERBS

Write the present, past, and past participle:

3.   A.   to run
     B.   to create
     C.   to do

SUBJECT / VERB:

Cross out prepositional phrase(s). Underline the subject once and the verb/verb phrase twice:

4.   During the morning, the dancers practiced outside the theater.

SENTENCE COMBINING:

5.   Furniture polish has been spilled on the carpeting.
     Peggy and Darrell are quickly trying to remove it.

DAY 102

CAPITALIZATION:

1.   last week's story "a trip with my family" was written for english class.

PUNCTUATION:

   Punctuate this envelope:

2._____

   Lynn Batt_____

   12 Trow St_____

   Plano Texas 75074_____

                                    Mr and Mrs Bob L Suite
                                    P O Box 34
                                    Peoria Arizona   85345

_____

PARTS OF SPEECH: ADJECTIVES

   Select any adjective(s) telling how many:

3.   The six children waded in some puddles.

PARTS OF SPEECH: ADVERBS

   Select any adverb(s) telling when:

4.   Yesterday Bill said, "See you later."

SENTENCE COMBINING:

5.   The street lights are on.
      The children must come in now.

CAPITALIZATION:

1.   the r. r. bowker co. is located on seventeenth street in new york.

PUNCTUATION:

Punctuate these titles:

2.   A.   (report)   Your Muscles
      B.   (movie)   Benji
      C.   (newspaper)   Los Angeles Times
      D.   (newspaper article)   Boating

SUBJECT / VERB:

Cross out prepositional phrase(s). Underline the subject once and the verb/verb phrase twice.

3.   In the afternoon, the girl and her dog ran.

SENTENCE TYPES:

Determine the type of sentence:

4.   A.   Come with us.
      B.   Water was drained from the tub.
      C.   It's over!

SENTENCE COMBINING:

5.   An actress played the part of Juliet.
      The actress is my sister.

DAY 104

CAPITALIZATION:

1.   the dons club* visited sierra elementary school.

          * name of club

PUNCTUATION:

2.   Jack said   Theres that old fashioned trolley

PARTS OF SPEECH: NOUNS

   Write a proper noun for each common noun:

3.   A.   town   C.   church   E.   country
      B.   person   D.   state   F.   business

PARTS OF SPEECH: VERBS

   Write the present, past, and past participle of the infinitive:

4.   A.   **to laugh**
      B.   **to speak**

SENTENCE COMBINING:

5.   The cat purred.
      The cat meowed.
      The cat darted across the street.

CAPITALIZATION:

1.   for reading class, kim read <u>tales of a fourth grade nothing</u>.

PUNCTUATION:

   Punctuate this friendly letter:

2.
                                                31 Core Dr
                                                Birmingham Alabama 35223
                                                Sept 27   19--

      Dear Ted

            Ill be home for Thanksgiving because Im paying half fare

                                                Sincerely
                                                Bart

PARTS OF SPEECH:

3.   What part of speech is **"Yeah!"**?

PARTS OF SPEECH: ADJECTIVES

   Select the correct adjective form:

4.   Shane is (taller, tallest) than his sister.

SENTENCE COMBINING:

5.   Jan is our school's fastest runner.
      Jan is on our track team.

DAY 106

CAPITALIZATION:

1.   when professor jamit came to our school, he talked about the arctic ocean.

PUNCTUATION:

2.   Yeah   Were on our way to Richmond Virginia for a week

PARTS OF SPEECH: ADVERBS

  Select the correct word:

3.   Kyle doesn't have _____ (any, no) marbles.

PARTS OF SPEECH: NOUNS

  Write the plural:

4.   A.   deer   C.   bug   E.   plant
      B.   lady   D.   goose   F.   bunch

SENTENCE COMBINING:

5.   The wagon is green.
      The wagon is for hay.
      The wagon is being pulled by two horses.

CAPITALIZATION:

1. the rocky mountains are in the west* .

    * region of the country

PUNCTUATION:

2. A. (poem)   McDingle McSquire
    B. (book)   Fred the Frog
    C. (story)   The Flying Dwarf
    D. (magazine article)   Sleep

DIRECT OBJECTS:

Cross out prepositional phrase(s). Underline the subject once and the verb/verb phrase twice. Label any direct object(s).

3. Jay had hit the ball to first base.

PARTS OF SPEECH: NOUNS

4. Add **es** to form the plural of nouns ending in _____, _____, _____, _____, and _____.

SENTENCE COMBINING:

5. Diana dropped a glass.
    The glass did not break.

DAY 108

CAPITALIZATION:

1.   the belville fire department held a labor day weekend fair.

PUNCTUATION:

2.   Larry exclaimed Yeah   Were going in one half hour

PARTS OF SPEECH: VERBS

  Select the correct verb;   underline the verb phrase twice:

3.   Tim must have _____ (threw, thrown) the ball.

PARTS OF SPEECH: PRONOUNS

4.   List all the possessive (ownership) pronouns.

SENTENCE COMBINING:

5.   The chair is broken.
      The chair is made of wood.
      The chair is also yellow.

CAPITALIZATION:

1.   did mother study about pocahontas in her history class?

PUNCTUATION:

2.   The Rev Capp finished his sermon and the people departed

PARTS OF SPEECH: VERBS

Select the correct verb;   underline the verb phrase twice:

3.   He could not have _____ (seen, saw) that.

FRIENDLY LETTER: ENVELOPE

 Write a return address:

4.   _____

        _____

        _____

        _____

                                            Ms. J. Lipp
                                            46 Doe Road
                                            Denver Colorado   88527

        _____

SENTENCE COMBINING:

5.   Twenty stories were entered in the contest.
        Paula's was chosen the winner.

DAY 110

CAPITALIZATION:

1.   the college student studied the shinto religion of japan.

PUNCTUATION:

2.   Stephanies dad lives at 23 Cobb Lane Memphis Tennessee

PARTS OF SPEECH: VERBS

  Select the correct verb;   underline the verb phrase twice:

3.   The boy should have _____ (brung, brought) his lunch.

PARTS OF SPEECH: CONJUNCTIONS

4.   The three coordinating conjunctions are _____, _____, and _____.

SENTENCE COMBINING:

5.   The dance is tonight.
      Joanna is not going.
      Joanna is going to a friend's house.

CAPITALIZATION:

Capitalize these titles:

1.   A.   <u>the door in the way</u>
      B.   <u>go jump in the pool</u>
      C.   <u>our roommate is missing</u>

PUNCTUATION:

2.   Susan your dog is cute friendly and frisky

PARTS OF SPEECH: NOUNS

Form the possessive:

3.   cups belonging to Mother

SENTENCE TYPES:

Determine the type of sentence:

4.   A.   I'm finished.
      B.   Take this.
      C.   We're leaving!

SENTENCE COMBINING:

5.   The chef made soup.
      The chef made a pie.
      The chef made potato salad.

DAY 112

CAPITALIZATION:

1. has senator jim fann spoken to the kiwanis club* lately?

      * name of club

PUNCTUATION:

Punctuate these titles:

2. A. (book)   What Spot?
    B. (story)   The Penguin
    C. (poem)   Pirate
    D. (magazine) Jack and Jill

PARTS OF SPEECH: NOUNS

Write the possessive form:

3. a dog belonging to two girls

PARTS OF SPEECH: ADJECTIVES

Select any adjective(s) telling how many:

4. On the third pitch, two runners stole base.

SENTENCE COMBINING:

5. The tray is silver.
    Grandma gave it to Judy.
    The tray has tarnished.

CAPITALIZATION:

1.   last night brenda said, "they visited the golden gate bridge."

PUNCTUATION:

2.   On Thurs December 12th we will arrive in Lansing Michigan

SUBJECT / VERB:

Cross out prepositional phrase(s). Underline the subject once and the verb/verb phrase twice:

3.   Jan finished her speech and sat down behind the podium.

SENTENCE TYPES:

Write the type of sentence:

4.   A.   Your advice is good.
        B.   Take this.
        C.   Is your seat belt fastened?

SENTENCE COMBINING:

5.   The plant dropped its leaves.
        New leaves then appeared.

DAY 114

CAPITALIZATION:

1. in washington, d. c., alex went to the jefferson memorial.

PUNCTUATION:

2. Yes Im going to Miami Florida in the morning

PARTS OF SPEECH: PRONOUNS

  Select the correct pronoun:

3. Do you know if (its, it's) Monday?

PARTS OF SPEECH: ADVERBS / ADJECTIVES

  Select the correct word:

4. Janet drives (slow, slowly).

SENTENCE COMBINING:

5. Mark is a dentist.
    Mark's office is in Vitter Square.

CAPITALIZATION:

1. in february a st. valentine's party was held at kolb lodge.

PUNCTUATION:

2. On December 7 1941 there was an attack on Pearl Harbor Hawaii

PARTS OF SPEECH: ADVERBS

  Select the correct word:

3. Karen never takes (any, no) money with her.

PARTS OF SPEECH: NOUNS

  Capitalize any proper nouns:

4. A. railroad   C. teacher   E. fido
    B. reading railroad   D. dog   F. berwick school

SENTENCE COMBINING:

5. The Indian told a legend.
    The legend was about the tribe's first warrior.

DAY 116

CAPITALIZATION:

1.   a wedding was held at calvary methodist church in idaho.

PUNCTUATION:

2.   Shirley remarked By the way Ill take the early bus

PARTS OF SPEECH: PRONOUNS

   Select the correct pronoun:

3.   Don't bring (your, you're) math book.

PARTS OF SPEECH:

   Select the correct word:

4.   If (there, their, they're) ready, let's go.

SENTENCE COMBINING:

5.   The children played checkers.
        Matt was the winner.

DAY 117

CAPITALIZATION:

1.   is pike's peak outside of colorado springs in colorado?

PUNCTUATION:

2.   Kent isnt the answer twenty four and three fifths

PARTS OF SPEECH: PRONOUNS

   Write any possessive pronoun that will be suitable:

3.   Is that _____bike?

SUBJECT / VERB:

   Cross out prepositional phrase(s).   Underline the subject once and the verb/verb phrase twice:

4.   From July until August, the troop will camp out.

SENTENCE COMBINING:

5.   They went on a picnic in the forest.
      They picked up pine cones.

DAY 118

CAPITALIZATION:

1.   my aunt julie hiked in yellowstone national park recently.

PUNCTUATION:

2.   Did you Cindy see the sleek new boats

PARTS OF SPEECH: PRONOUNS

   Select the correct pronoun:

3.   Sheila and _____ (I, me) were chosen.

PARTS OF SPEECH: ADJECTIVES

   Select any adjective(s):

4.   A happy, laughing child sang funny songs.

SENTENCE COMBINING:

5.   The girl is water-skiing.
      This is her first time.

CAPITALIZATION:

1.   in the 1960's, president kennedy toured a civil war battleground.

PUNCTUATION:

2.   The ladies club meets at 12 Elm St Bangor Maine on Mondays

PARTS OF SPEECH: PRONOUN / ADJECTIVE

   Determine if the underlined word is serving as an adjective or as a pronoun:

3.   A.   I like <u>that.</u>
       B.   I like <u>that</u> hat.

SUBJECT / VERB:

   Cross out prepositional phrase(s).   Underline the subject once and the verb/verb phrase twice:

4.   A brown mouse ran through the hallway and sneezed.

SENTENCE COMBINING:

5.   Their father is a policeman.
       Their father works the night shift.

DAY 120

CAPITALIZATION:

1.   has jane's father flown on american airlines lately?

PUNCTUATION:

2.   Hes usually calm cool and collected

PARTS OF SPEECH: ADVERBS

  Select any adverb(s) telling <u>when</u> or <u>where</u>:

3.   Often Martin walks there with his dad.

PARTS OF SPEECH: PREPOSITIONS

  Select any object(s) of the preposition:

4.   By noon on Friday, the check must be in the mail.

SENTENCE COMBINING:

5.   Charles went to a store.
      It was a grocery store.
      Charles bought popsicles.

CAPITALIZATION:

1.   is jacob lawrence's painting called "the migration of the negro"?

PUNCTUATION:

2.   Yes theyll spend the night and well serve breakfast

PARTS OF SPEECH: NOUNS

  Select any noun(s):

3.   Three cars sped around the raceway during the last lap.

SENTENCE   TYPES:

  Determine the type of sentence:

4.   A.   Dad is home.
     B.   Dad is home!
     C.   Is Dad home?
     D.   Dad, come home.

SENTENCE   COMBINING:

5.   The band marched down Main Street.
     The band was composed of children.
     The leader was the mayor.

DAY 122

CAPITALIZATION:

Capitalize the heading and greeting of this letter:

1.
                                    77 lark drive
                                    lancaster, kentucky   40446
                                    january 13, 19--

my favorite cousin,

PUNCTUATION:

2.   Your name appeared on the list in fact as Jacobs Ken C

PARTS OF SPEECH: ADJECTIVE / ADVERB

Select the correct word:

3.   The clown juggles   (easy, easily) .

PARTS OF SPEECH: ADVERBS

4.   The seven adverbs that tell **to what extent** are _____, _____,
       _____, _____, _____, _____, and _____.

SENTENCE COMBINING:

5.   The family had a garage sale.
       The family sold an old bike.
       The bike sold for twenty dollars.

CAPITALIZATION:

1.   either uncle dale or i will take united airlines flight 106.

PUNCTUATION:

2.   Our new address is 100 N Link Ave Wichita Kansas

PARTS OF SPEECH:

  Select the correct word:

3.   A.   (You're, Your) the winner.
       B.   The boys are going with (they're, their, there) leader.

PARTS OF SPEECH: ADVERBS

  Select the correct adverb:

4.   Susan jumps (higher, highest) than I.

SENTENCE COMBINING:

5.   The children made sand castles on the beach.
       The teenagers played volleyball on the beach.

DAY 124

CAPITALIZATION:

1.   is babe ruth's statue in the baseball hall of fame in cooperstown?

PUNCTUATION:

 Punctuate this outline:

2.   I   Mountain chains
          A   Rockies
          B   Appalachians
      II   Rivers
          A   Colorado
          B   Rio Grande

PARTS OF SPEECH: PRONOUNS

3.   The pronouns that can be used as a subject are _____, _____, _____, _____, _____, _____, and _____.

SENTENCES / FRAGMENTS:

 **Determine if the group of words is a sentence or a fragment.
 Remember: a fragment does not have both subject and verb:**

4.   The swimmer thirty laps.

SENTENCE COMBINING:

5.   The pillow case is torn.
      The pillow case is blue with flowers.

CAPITALIZATION:

1.   a rocky seashore runs along acadia national park in maine.

PUNCTUATION:

2.   Dr Tarn and his wife went to an A M A* meeting July 21 1970 in Ohio

         * abbreviation for American Medical Association

PARTS OF SPEECH: PRONOUNS

   Select the correct pronoun:

3.   The custodian went with Wyatt and _____ (he, him) .

PARTS OF SPEECH: ADJECTIVES

   Select the correct adjective:

4.   This typewriter is (gooder, better) than that one.

SENTENCE COMBINING:

5.   Joyce is a gymnast.
     Her specialty is tumbling.

DAY 126

CAPITALIZATION:

1.   a replica of an 1870 town called lumbertown, u. s. a., is in minnesota.

PUNCTUATION:

2.   I like dancing better replied Toms friend

PARTS OF SPEECH: VERBS

Write the present, past, and past participle of the infinitive:

3.   A.   **to ride**
        B.   **to do**
        C.   **to take**

PARTS OF SPEECH: ADJECTIVES

Select any adjective(s):

4.   Seven hungry cows ate the green leafy grass.

SENTENCE COMBINING:

5.   We went to a circus.
        We saw a lion jump through a ring.

CAPITALIZATION:

Capitalize these titles:

1.   A.   "old king cole"
      B.   <u>the velveteen rabbit</u>
      C.   <u>eight is enough</u>
      D.   <u>where the red fern grows</u>

PUNCTUATION:

2.   No youre not taking Spencers snake with you

PARTS OF SPEECH: ADJECTIVES
   Select any adjective(s):

3.   A quick brown fox jumped over the lazy dog.

PARTS OF SPEECH: NOUNS

   Write the plural:

4.   A.   pet   C.   moose   E.   box
      B.   child   D.   recess   F.   memory

SENTENCE COMBINING:

5.   The rocking horse is painted blue.
      Jeremy is riding it.

DAY 128

CAPITALIZATION:

1.   some russian cosmonauts attended a white house* dinner.

       name of special house for Presidents

PUNCTUATION:

Punctuate this letter:

2.   (A)   66 Lincoln Drive
                                        Whittier CA 90607
                                        Sept 22 19--

     (B)   Dear Joan

     (C)   Our twenty one friends will be arriving in
           Tulsa Oklahoma in October

                                 (D)   Sincerely
                                 (E)   Marsha

FRIENDLY LETTER:

3.   The parts of a friendly letter are: (A)_____, (B)_____,
     (C)_____, (D)_____, and (E)_____.

PARTS OF SPEECH: VERBS

Select the correct verb; underline the verb phrase twice:

4.   That player should have _____ (stole, stolen) home.

SENTENCE COMBINING:

5.   His father writes stories about animals.
     His mother writes stories about cooking.

CAPITALIZATION:

Capitalize these titles:

1.　A.　"all summer in a day"
　　B.　<u>the merchant of venice</u>
　　C.　"why nobody pets the lion at the zoo"
　　D.　"stopping by woods on a snowy evening"

PUNCTUATION:

2.　Jodys brother however draws horses cats and dogs

PARTS OF SPEECH:　NOUNS

Write the possessive form:

3.　several plates belonging to Chris

PARTS OF SPEECH:

4.　List the 23 helping (auxiliary) verbs.

SENTENCE COMBINING:

5.　The play begins in ten minutes.
　　The play begins at eight o'clock.

DAY 130

CAPITALIZATION:

1.   according to <u>genesis</u>* in the <u>bible</u>, jacob's gift to joseph was a coat.

            * name of book

PUNCTUATION:

Punctuate these titles:

2.   A.   (song)   America the Beautiful
       B.   (movie)   The Wizard of Oz
       C.   (book)   Tex
       D.   (magazine) Field and Stream

PARTS OF SPEECH: VERBS

Select the correct verb:

3.   This lady often (eats, eat) only vegetables.

PARTS OF SPEECH: ADVERBS

Select any adverb(s):

4.   Recently birds flew in and out among the trees.

SENTENCE COMBINING:

5.   The sky was blue in the morning.
       In the afternoon it rained.

CAPITALIZATION:

1.   a hindu temple was erected near new delhi*, india.

          * name of city

PUNCTUATION:

2.   The companys address is P O Box 43 New York N Y

PARTS OF SPEECH:

  Select the correct word:

3.   A.   (Too, To, Two) answers were given.
       B.   I want to visit (their, there, they're) soon.

SUBJECT / VERB:

  Cross out prepositional phrase(s). Underline the subject once and the verb/verb phrase twice:

4.   The secretary of the club has introduced the treasurer.

SENTENCE COMBINING:

5.   Penguins waddled across the snow.
       Penguins also jumped into the water.

DAY 132

CAPITALIZATION:

1.   the wabash travel agency* booked an alaskan cruise last spring.

          * name of a business

PUNCTUATION:

Punctuate these titles:

2.   A.   (short story) Thirteen
      B.   (magazine)   Sports Illustrated
      C.   (ship)   U.S.S. Constitution

PARTS OF SPEECH: NOUNS

Capitalize proper nouns:

3.   A.   gloves   C.   anderson house restaurant
      B.   markin theater D.   movie theater

PARTS OF SPEECH: INTERJECTIONS

4.   Give an example of an interjection.

SENTENCE COMBINING:

5.   There are six lights in the kitchen.
      One of the lights is burned out.

CAPITALIZATION:

1.   a boston church was erected near the hilton hotel last may.

PUNCTUATION:

Punctuate these titles:

2.   A.   (book)   Our Family Tree
      B.   (poem)   I'm Nobody
      C.   (magazine article) Bingo
      D.   (newspaper)   Gettysburg Times

PARTS OF SPEECH: ADVERBS

Select adverb(s) telling <u>when</u> or <u>where</u>:

3.   Eventually the girls went inside for a short time.

PARTS OF SPEECH: ADJECTIVES / PRONOUNS

Determine if the underlined word is used as an adjective or as a pronoun:

4.   A.   <u>Those</u> trees are being trimmed.
      B.   Are <u>those</u> yours?

SENTENCE COMBINING:

5.   The turkey was sliced.
      The turkey was placed in sandwiches.
      The turkey was barbecued.

DAY 134

CAPITALIZATION:

1.   their race car was entered in the daytona 500 for goodyear company.

PUNCTUATION:

2.   Yes you may read Johns essay entitled My Vacation

PARTS OF SPEECH: CONJUNCTIONS

3.   The three coordinating conjunctions are _____, _____, and _____.

PARTS OF SPEECH: VERBS

  Select the correct verb:

4.   Several dancers (don't , doesn't) have shoes.

SENTENCE COMBINING:

5.   Jenny's friend is Lori.
       Lori won a short story contest.

CAPITALIZATION:

Capitalize these titles:

1.   A.   (painting)   <u>freedom of speech</u>
     B.   (book)   <u>the last of the mohicans</u>
     C.   (newspaper article)   "a day to remember"
     D.   (television show)   <u>the days of our lives</u>

PUNCTUATION:

2.   Our team for example scored thirty one points

PARTS OF SPEECH: PREPOSITIONS

Select the object(s) of the preposition(s):

3.   Down the lane and around the corner lives the mayor.

PARTS OF SPEECH: NOUNS

Write the possessive form:

4.   A.   a clock belonging to Uncle Kim and Aunt Edna
     B.   ducks belonging to Farmer Jones
     C.   cards belonging to our teacher

SENTENCE   COMBINING:

5.   Their car is gray.
     Their car is new.
     Their car has bucket seats.
     Their car has fancy tires.

DAY 136

CAPITALIZATION:

1. has attorney gill met with her client in an adams county jail?

PUNCTUATION:

2. One half of Carls grades were good but he failed math

PARTS OF SPEECH: VERBS

  Write the contraction:

3. A. we shall   C. they are   E. she is
    B. will not   D. would not   F. have not

PARTS OF SPEECH: ADJECTIVES / ADVERBS

  Select the correct answer:

4. I don't feel _____ (good, well) .

SENTENCE COMBINING:

5. The child misbehaved.
    The child threw herself on the floor.
    The child also screamed.

CAPITALIZATION:

Capitalize this letter:

1.
                                                            11 bow lane
                                                            phoenix, arizona   85015
                                                            december 1, 19--

   dear cousin louie,

        i saw disneyland last summer when visiting anaheim,
   california.

                                                            sincerely yours,
                                                            arnie t. bogs

PUNCTUATION:

2.   I believe Mr Dobbs that youre the last entrant

PARTS OF SPEECH: PRONOUNS

Select the correct pronoun:

3.   Both Mary and _____ (she, her) are deciding.

PARTS OF SPEECH: VERBS

Select the correct verb:

4.   One of the girls _____ (leave, leaves) on Friday.

SENTENCE COMBINING:

5.   The clothes are still damp.
       The clothes have been in the dryer for thirty minutes.

DAY 138

CAPITALIZATION:

1.   is vista international hotel located on penn avenue in pittsburgh?

PUNCTUATION:

2.   An ex marine delivered a long political speech

PARTS OF SPEECH: ADJECTIVES / PRONOUNS

   Determine if the underlined word serves as an adjective or as a pronoun:

3.   A.   I like <u>that</u> coat.
     B.   <u>That</u> is her final offer.

PARTS OF SPEECH: NOUNS

4.   To form the plural of nouns ending in _____, _____, _____, _____, and _____, add **es**.

SENTENCE COMBINING:

5.   The shirts were wrinkled.
     The shirts had been stuffed in a suitcase.

CAPITALIZATION:

1.   during the ice age, the waters of the antarctic ocean were frozen.

PUNCTUATION:

Write the correct abbreviation:

2.   A.   foot   C.   inches   E.   Road
      B.   pound   D.   after noon   F.   meter
                                (post meridian)

PARTS OF SPEECH: ADJECTIVES

Select the correct form:

3.   Jill is the _____ (best, better) runner of the two.

PARTS OF SPEECH: PRONOUNS

Select the correct pronoun:

4.   The dog jumped on _____ (him, he) constantly.

SENTENCE COMBINING:

5.   Place your name in the right hand corner of the paper.
      Below that, place the date.

DAY 140

CAPITALIZATION:

1.   at russell's tavern* near gettysburg, president george washington stayed.

          * name of inn

PUNCTUATION:

2.   On Tuesday June 6 1940 my fathers friend married

PARTS OF SPEECH: NOUNS

   Determine if the noun is concrete or abstract:

3.   A.   buffalo   C.   honesty   E.   love
       B.   garbage   D.   canal   F.   wisdom

PARTS OF SPEECH: VERBS

   Write the correct contraction:

4.   A.   must not   C.   I would   E.   cannot
       B.   you will   D.   what is   F.   would not

SENTENCE COMBINING:

5.   Tad's bike is blue.
       Tad's bike was a birthday gift.
       The bike is a racer.

CAPITALIZATION:

1.   they bought swiss cheese and english muffins at miracle market*.

   * name of grocery store

PUNCTUATION:

2.   Sophia said Were flying there and well return by train

PARTS OF SPEECH: PRONOUNS

Select the correct word:

3.   (Who's, Whose) on first base?

PARTS OF SPEECH: NOUNS

Determine if the word is a common noun or a proper noun:

4.   A.   book   C.   Duke   E.   canary
     B.   tape   D.   bird   F.   Canada

SENTENCE COMBINING:

5.   The coin is old.
     The coin is gold.
     The coin is valuable.

DAY 142

CAPITALIZATION:

1.   the jewish people were led out of egypt* by moses.

         * name of a country

PUNCTUATION:

2.   Ms Davis asked Wheres your car Vicki

PARTS OF SPEECH: VERBS

   Select the correct verb;   underline the verb phrase twice:

3.   The kitten must have _____ (drank, drunk) the milk.

PARTS OF SPEECH: ADJECTIVES / PRONOUNS

   Determine if the underlined word is an adjective or a pronoun:

4.   A.   <u>Many</u> ribbons were won.
      B.   <u>Many</u> of the flowers bloomed.

SENTENCE COMBINING:

5.   The child crossed the street.
      The child first looked both ways.

CAPITALIZATION:

1.   a lutheran church is located at the base of moon mountain.

PUNCTUATION:

2.   Dads company is located at 42 Dee Rd Atlanta Georgia 30345

PARTS OF SPEECH: PRONOUNS

   Select the correct pronoun:

3.   The winner was _____ (I, me).

SENTENCE TYPES:

   Determine the type of sentence:

4.   A.   Is it raining?
      B.   It is raining.
      C.   It's raining!

SENTENCE COMBINING:

5.   The television was turned on.
      The show was about history.
      Brian was watching it.

DAY 144

CAPITALIZATION:

1.   a quilt entitled "fair grounds" is at the smithsonian institution's renwick gallery.

PUNCTUATION:

2.   A gentle cool breeze blew across the run down sailboat

PARTS OF SPEECH: VERBS

   Write the present, past, and past participle:

3.   A.   **to run**
       B.   **to eat**
       C.   **to see**

PARTS OF SPEECH: ADJECTIVES / ADVERBS

   Select the correct word:

4.   The girls played _____ (good, well) .

SENTENCE COMBINING:

5.   The couple went water-skiing.
       The lady drove the boat.
       The man skied.

CAPITALIZATION:

1.   the hopi indians of the southwest make beautiful jewelry.

PUNCTUATION:

2.   The Hudson Riv area of N Y is a lovely fertile region

FRIENDLY LETTER:

3.   Write a return address; you are the letter sender.

_____

_____

_____

_____

_____

PARTS OF SPEECH: NOUNS

   Select noun(s):

4.   Mandy took pens, pencils, and a notebook with her.

SENTENCE COMBINING:

5.   The present was wrapped in blue paper.
      The present had a white bow.
      The present was for June.

DAY 146

CAPITALIZATION:

1.   a biglerville policeman was taken to memorial hospital on tuesday.

PUNCTUATION:

2.   Its raining today and Ive without a doubt forgotten my umbrella

PARTS OF SPEECH: PRONOUNS

   **Select the word to which the pronoun refers back.   This is
   called an antecedent:**

3.   The dog wagged <u>its</u> tail.

SUBJECTS / VERBS:

   **Cross out prepositional phrase(s).   Underline the subject once
   and the verb/verb phrase twice:**

4.   The plumber in the red hat talked and fixed our faucet.

SENTENCE COMBINING:

5.   The sunglasses are on the counter.
       The sunglasses belong to Jim.
       The counter is tiled.

CAPITALIZATION:

1.   last summer captain doug bayn visited the astrodome in houston.

PUNCTUATION:

2.   I love it   exclaimed Nikki

DIRECT OBJECTS:

   Underline the subject once and the verb/verb phrase twice.
   Label the direct object(s):

3.   A horse ate an apple.

PARTS OF SPEECH:

   Select the correct answer:

4.   A.   Is Jody (to, two, too) years old?
        B.   Is (there, they're, their) favorite ice cream served?
        C.   Did you (hear, here) the good news?

SENTENCE COMBINING:

5.   Lori took a trip.
        Lori went to England.
        Lori went with her grandmother.

DAY 148

CAPITALIZATION:

1.   the mayor and senator gert dined at a san francisco hotel.

PUNCTUATION:

2.   The bright shining light cast its glow on the ex marines car

PARTS OF SPEECH: NOUNS

  Write the plural:

3.   A.   dish   C.   sheep   E.   child
      B.   friend   D.   class   F.   mother-in-law

PARTS OF SPEECH: ADJECTIVES

  Select the correct form:

4.   This barber is (more eager, most eager) than his partner.

SENTENCE COMBINING:

5.   The dog is a St. Bernard.
      The dog is friendly.
      The dog often jumps over the fence.

CAPITALIZATION:

1.   the movie <u>snow white and the seven dwarfs</u> was playing at tri-theater.

PUNCTUATION:

2.   Marys dad her uncle and her cousin went to Bangor Maine yesterday

PART OF SPEECH: VERBS

  Select the correct verb:

3.   The barrels in the arena (falls, fall) over.

PARTS OF SPEECH: ADVERBS

  Select the correct word:

4.   One girl never has (no, any) tennis balls.

SENTENCE COMBINING:

5.   The bicycle was in the driveway.
      The bicycle belongs to Janis.
      The driveway is at the school.

DAY 150

CAPITALIZATION:

1.   does the march of dimes association send out easter seals?

PUNCTUATION:

2.   Two thirds of the class went to Brians party

PARTS OF SPEECH: PRONOUNS

   Select the correct pronoun:

3.   Some trees had lost _____ (its, their) leaves.

PARTS OF SPEECH: ADVERBS

   Select adverbs. REMEMBER: Adverbs tell <u>when</u>, <u>where</u>, <u>how</u>, and <u>to what extent</u>:

4.   First, let's go outside to play; afterwards, we can eat.

SENTENCE COMBINING:

5.   The copy machine is broken.
      A paper is jammed in the machine.
      Ms. Sax is repairing it.

CAPITALIZATION:

1.   is the tournament of roses parade held in pasadena each year?

PUNCTUATION:

2.   Because dinner wasnt prepared we didnt leave until 7 00 P M

PARTS OF SPEECH: VERBS

  Select the correct verb:

3.   A.   Harriet (sets, sits) food on the table.

      B.   The mother (lay, laid) the tile in her kitchen.

PARTS OF SPEECH: PREPOSITIONS

  Cross out prepositional phrase(s). Underline the subject once and the verb/verb phrase twice:

4.   Sal wants to go with Jerry and me.

SENTENCE COMBINING:

5.   Two hamsters are in a cage.
      One hamster is drinking water.
      Another hamster darts around the cage.

DAY 152

CAPITALIZATION:

1.   a christian festivity is the celebration of christ's birth in bethlehem.

PUNCTUATION:

2.   No I dont believe that June 1 1919 is the answer

PARTS OF SPEECH: ADVERBS

  Select adverb(s):

3.   Boldly the winner ran inside for a very short speech.

PARTS OF SPEECH: NOUNS

  Select noun(s):

4.   Martha's friend is a chef at a resort near her house.

SENTENCE COMBINING:

5.   Jane is angry.
     Jane is silent.
     Jane left the room.

CAPITALIZATION:

1.   an arthritis* patient saw dr. lang in her office at smith medical building.

        * a disease

PUNCTUATION:

Punctuate these titles:

2.   A.   (book)   Suzanne
      B.   (ship)   Titanic
      C.   (chapter)   Writing
      D.   (magazine)   The Owl

PARTS OF SPEECH:

Write the present, past, and future tenses:

3.   A.   **to buy**
      B.   **to dance**

PARTS OF SPEECH: INTERJECTIONS

4.   Give an example of an interjection.

SENTENCE COMBINING:

5.   Dr. Jobe is a veterinarian.
      Dr. Jobe vaccinates our cows.

DAY 154

CAPITALIZATION:

1.   the sierra madre mountains are in the west.

PUNCTUATION:

2.   Yeah   Our team scored twenty five points exclaimed Aaron

PARTS OF SPEECH: PRONOUNS

   Select the correct pronoun:

3.   The last contestants were Debbie and _____ (I, me) .

SUBJECT / VERB:

   Cross out prepositional phrase(s). Underline the subject once and the verb/verb phrase twice:

4.   Each of the dancers performed and then bowed.

SENTENCE COMBINING:

5.   Daren is a tumbler.
      Daren competes in state tournaments.
      Daren often wins.

CAPITALIZATION:

1.　does professor kelly teach reading or english at that middle school?

PUNCTUATION:

Punctuate these titles:

2.　A.　(movie)　　　　Fiddler on the Roof
　　B.　(book)　　　　Japan's People
　　C.　(magazine article)　Your Hair
　　D.　(poem)　　　　Evangeline

FRIENDLY LETTERS:

3.　Write the heading of a friendly letter.

PARTS OF SPEECH:　PREPOSITIONS / ADVERBS

Determine if the underlined word serves as a preposition or as an adverb:

4.　A.　The squirrel looked up.
　　B.　The children ran up the stairs.

SENTENCE COMBINING:

5.　The lady screamed.
　　The lady was in the grocery store.
　　The lady said that her purse had been stolen.

DAY 156

CAPITALIZATION:

1.   later, judge worth arrived at the u. s. capitol for a tour.

PUNCTUATION:

2.   Phil asked Wheres the non fiction book Greg

PARTS OF SPEECH: NOUNS

3.   Three examples of abstract nouns are _____, _____, and _____.

PARTS OF SPEECH: ADJECTIVES

   Select adjectives:

4.   Two young ladies scooped water from that sinking boat.

SENTENCE COMBINING:

5.   A new restaurant opened.
       Doug's brother works there.
       Doug's brother is a waiter.

CAPITALIZATION:

1.   during his trip to the orient,* did sam see the great wall** of china?

         * region of the world
         **historical landmark

PUNCTUATION:

2.   Her ex boyfriend works and attends college

SENTENCES / FRAGMENTS:

Determine if the group of words is a sentence or a fragment.
REMEMBER: A fragment usually is missing a subject or a verb.

3.   Running down the road.

FRIENDLY LETTERS:

Label the parts of this friendly letter:

4.
                                        9 Dow Drive
                    (A)   Peoria, Arizona   85345
                                        March 2, 19--

     (B)   Dear Friend,
     (C)   Your new book should be arriving soon.

                         (D)   Sincerely,
                         (E)   Nicole

SENTENCE COMBINING:

5.   The floors are wooden.
        The floors are stained.
        The floors need to be sanded.

DAY 158

CAPITALIZATION:

Capitalize this friendly letter:

> 2 cree street
> glendale arizona   85306
> july 3 19--

my dear aunt

lets meet in picadilly square in london england in may

> your niece
> tonya

PUNCTUATION:

2.   Punctuate the above friendly letter:

PARTS OF SPEECH: ADVERBS

 Select adverbs.   REMEMBER: Adverbs tell <u>how</u>, <u>when</u>, <u>where</u>, and <u>to what extent</u>:

3.   We always stay here when in North Dakota.

PARTS OF SPEECH: NOUNS

 Write the possessive:

4.   a fountain belonging to Brett and Tina

SENTENCE COMBINING:

5.   The group hiked for three hours.
      The group hiked into a canyon.
      The group ate lunch there.

CAPITALIZATION:

1.   did captain jones meet with the president* at camp david?

                    * of the United States

PUNCTUATION:

2.   An airplane called the Spruce Goose is at Long Beach California
      I believe

PARTS OF SPEECH: PREPOSITIONS:

   Select object(s) of the prepositions:

3.   Within two hours the swelling of the ankle had gone down.

SENTENCE TYPES:

   Determine the type of sentence:

4.   A.   Stand up.
      B.   He's leaving.
      C.   Will you remember?

SENTENCE COMBINING:

5.   Martha talks loudly.
      Martha's sister is very quiet.

DAY 160

CAPITALIZATION:

1.   a group from germany toured lincoln memorial and the u. s. senate.

PUNCTUATION:

2.   The U S S Constitution in Boston Massachusetts is historical

PARTS OF SPEECH:

  Select the correct word:

3.   A.   The waiters left (their, there, they're) jobs early.
      B.   (Two, Too, To) much snow fell.
      C.   I (here, hear) you.

PARTS OF SPEECH: VERBS

  Write the present, past, and past participle:

4.   A.   **to lie** (meaning to rest)
      B.   **to start**

SENTENCE COMBINING:

5.   Sherry purchased popcorn.
      The popcorn was in a bag.
      The popcorn was unsalted.

CAPITALIZATION:

1.   a student at lakewood middle school received a polio vaccine.

PUNCTUATION:

2.   Three fourths of Lauras friends I think were there

FRIENDLY LETTERS: ENVELOPE

**Write your return address and address the envelope to a friend.
(If you do not know a friend's address, make one up!)**

3./4.

_____
_____
_____
_____

                              _____
                              _____
                              _____

_____

SENTENCE COMBINING:

5.   Dark clouds rolled in.
        Some rain began to fall.
        The rain fell for an hour.

DAY 162

CAPITALIZATION:

1.   the french driver turned north near opoe store in cherry valley.

PUNCTUATION:

2.   Sandys car her bike and her dog are in the familys garage

PARTS OF SPEECH: VERBS

   Select the correct verb:

3.   Her mother and dad _____ (race, races).

PARTS OF SPEECH: NOUNS

   Determine if the noun is common or proper:

4.   A.   club   C.   hillcrest country club   E.   canary
      B.   country club   D.   bird   F.   tweety bird

SENTENCE COMBINING:

5.   The car is white.
      The car was speeding.
      The car has a dent in it.

CAPITALIZATION:

1.   at delgado's pizza house,* the italian sandwiches are good.

             * name of a restaurant

PUNCTUATION:

   Punctuate these titles:

2.   A.   (book)   How to Eat Fried Worms
        B.   (story)   The Gift of the Magi
        C.   (play)   Annie
        D.   (song)   Daisy

PARTS OF SPEECH: NOUNS / PRONOUNS

   Determine if the word is a noun or a pronoun:

3.   A.   girl   C.   her   E.   we
        B.   me   D.   boat   F.   pie

PARTS OF SPEECH: ADVERBS

   **Select adverb(s).   REMEMBER: Adverbs tell <u>how</u>, <u>when</u>, <u>where</u>,
   and <u>to what extent</u>:**

4.   Yesterday, a tired camel knelt down so gently.

SENTENCE COMBINING:

5.   The air is filled with smoke.
        A brush fire is burning.

DAY 164

CAPITALIZATION:

1.   after the ice age, asian hunters crossed the bering strait.

PUNCTUATION:

2.   Mr and Mrs Jacobs sell the following   yogurt ice cream and milk

PARTS OF SPEECH: VERBS

   Write the present, past, and past participle:

3.   A.   **to lie**   (meaning to rest)
      B.   **to smile**
      C.   **to see**
      D.   **to grow**

PARTS OF SPEECH: PRONOUNS

   Reflexive pronouns end with <u>self</u> or <u>selves</u>.

4.   Give an example of a reflexive pronoun.

SENTENCE COMBINING:

5.   Before lunch, they shopped.
      They shopped at a new mall.
      They bought sweaters.

CAPITALIZATION:

1.   when harold's parents went to europe,* they saw the eiffel tower, the leaning tower of pisa, and a swiss play.

        * name of a continent

PUNCTUATION:

2.   Wow   Hes enclosed one half of Ralphs collection   exclaimed Judy

PARTS OF SPEECH: NOUNS

Determine if the noun is concrete or abstract:

3.   A.   kindness   C.   fear   E.   cream
      B.   candles   D.   beauty   F.   air

PARTS OF SPEECH: PRONOUNS

Interrogative pronouns ask a question:

4.   Write an interrogative pronoun.

SENTENCE COMBINING:

5.   A security guard searched the parking lot.
      A security guard was looking for a stolen wallet.
      The wallet was not found.

DAY 166

CAPITALIZATION:

1.   for breakfast, she ate canadian bacon, kellogg's corn flakes, and a danish pastry.

PUNCTUATION:

2.   The answer I think isnt twenty three Lois

PARTS OF SPEECH: PRONOUNS / ADJECTIVES

Determine if the underlined word serves as a pronoun or as an adjective:

3.   A.   <u>Both</u> ended the discussion.
      B.   Have <u>both</u> adults entered the tournament?

PARTS OF SPEECH: VERBS

Write the present tense, past tense, and future tense:

4.   A.   **to rise**
      B.   **to draw**
      C.   **to dance**

SENTENCE COMBINING:

5.   A lady washed her car.
      No one helped her.
      Her car was new.

CAPITALIZATION:

1.   mrs. r. dil studied the hindu religion at santa ana college.

PUNCTUATION:

2.   No Lee we arent   said Tara   leaving for Boise Idaho today

PARTS OF SPEECH: NOUNS

Write the possessive:

3.   A.   a meeting of painters
      B.   a master of more than one ox
      C.   sofas belonging to Chris
      D.   the color of a vase

PARTS OF SPEECH: ADJECTIVES

Select the correct form:

4.   This stairway is (closest, closer) than that one.

SENTENCE COMBINING:

5.   Sandy watched television.
      Gregory drew a picture.
      Jana also drew a picture.

DAY 168

CAPITALIZATION:

1.   is fingal's cave located on staffa island off western scotland*?

          * name of country

PUNCTUATION:

2.   Although two fifths of the children didnt go the picnic was fun

PARTS OF SPEECH: ADJECTIVES

  Select adjectives:

3.   The large, walnut sundae was served on a round, silver tray.

PARTS OF SPEECH: ADVERBS

  Write the comparative (2) and superlative (3 or more) forms:

4.   A.   well
      B.   hard
      C.   eagerly

SENTENCE COMBINING:

5.   Their grass is brown.
      No one has watered it.
      It also has not rained recently.

CAPITALIZATION:

1.   the methodist church on brown street held a <u>bible</u> school.

PUNCTUATION:

2.   When the team had won the coaches treat was pizza and coke

PARTS OF SPEECH: NOUNS

Write the plural:

3.   A.   dash   C.   ring   E.   brother-in-law
      B.   calf   D.   louse   F.   cry

SENTENCES / FRAGMENTS:

Determine if the group of words is a sentence or a fragment:

4.   A.   Dressed in blue.
      B.   We'd rather stay here.

SENTENCE COMBINING:

5.   His lunch box is blue.
      His lunch box is shaped like a radio.
      The lunch box does not play music.

DAY 170

CAPITALIZATION:

1.   in spanish class, we studied about the inca indians of peru.

PUNCTUATION:

2.   Were you by the way born Jan 30 1980 in Toledo Ohio

PARTS OF SPEECH: NOUNS

  Write the possessive:

3.   a pig belonging to more than one child

SENTENCES / FRAGMENTS:

  Determine if the group of words is a sentence or a fragment:

4.   A.   Walking down the street.
       B.   The bus arrived early.
       C.   The ran in a race.
       D.   Come here.

SENTENCE COMBINING:

5.   Joel made an airplane.
       The airplane was of paper.
       Joel flew the airplane across the room.

DAY 171

CAPITALIZATION:

1.   during the american revolution, the tory party* favored england.

        * name of political party

PUNCTUATION:

2.   Yes her well mannered nephew arrived on the Icelandic**

        ** name of ship

PARTS OF SPEECH: ADJECTIVES

 Select the predicate adjective. REMEMBER: A predicate adjective occurs <u>after</u> the verb and describes the <u>subject</u>:

3.   Her hair grew long.

PARTS OF SPEECH: INTERJECTIONS

4.   Write three examples of interjections.

SENTENCE COMBINING:

5.   A fitness center opened yesterday.
      Myra joined.
      It is very expensive to join.

DAY 172

CAPITALIZATION:

1.   because of james madison's help with the <u>u. s. constitution</u>, he is
      called the "father of the constitution."

PUNCTUATION:

2.   Youre the best   the man announced   in this division

PARTS OF SPEECH: VERBS

   Select the correct verb; underline the verb phrase twice:

3.   A.   The dog had _____ (laid, lain) on the rug.
      B.   Lillian might have _____ (snuck, sneaked) home.
      C.   Has the lawyer _____ (brought, brung) her client?
      D.   Should we have _____ (saw, seen) that?

SUBJECTS / VERBS:

   **Cross out prepositional phrases. Underline the subject once
   and the verb or verb phrase twice:**

4.   One of the children ran to the gate and opened it.

SENTENCE COMBINING:

5.   The bicyclist stopped to rest.
      The bicyclist rested on a park bench.

CAPITALIZATION:

1.   in canton, ohio, you will find the pro football hall of fame.

PUNCTUATION:

2.   Jenny asked Wheres Jessicas note pad

PARTS OF SPEECH: VERBS

3.   List the 23 helping (auxiliary) verbs.

_____

_____

_____

PARTS OF SPEECH: CONJUNCTIONS

Select any coordinating conjunction:

4.   The coke and pizza were ordered but not eaten.

SENTENCE COMBINING:

5.   The belt buckle is engraved.
      The belt buckle is made of silver.
      The belt buckle belongs to a rancher.

DAY 174

CAPITALIZATION:

1.   duane went to fort ticonderoga, an american revolution fort.

PUNCTUATION:

2.   Youre right   the clerk said   and Ill exchange it

PARTS OF SPEECH: ADVERBS

3.   The seven adverbs that tell **to what extent** are _____, _____, _____,
       _____, _____, _____, and _____.

PARTS OF SPEECH: VERBS

   Write the contraction:

4.   A.   does not   C.   who is   E.   will not
       B.   we will   D.   cannot   F.   I have

SENTENCE COMBINING:

5.   Joe walked to the drugstore.
       Joe bought gum drops.
       Joe also bought licorice and crackers.

CAPITALIZATION:

1.   a child with german measles played chess and read <u>moby dick</u>.

PUNCTUATION:

2.   When Barbs uncle visits he often brings pasta bread or sausage

PARTS OF SPEECH: ADVERBS

  Select the correct form:

3.   Of the three trains, the <u>Rob Express</u> travels (more slowly, most slowly).

PARTS OF SPEECH: ADJECTIVES

  Select adjective(s):

4.   Those happy winners held up large, gold trophies.

SENTENCE COMBINING:

5.   The pan is oblong.
      The pan is used for roasting.
      Mrs. Delany is cooking a turkey in the pan.

DAY 176

CAPITALIZATION:

1.   the cann family planted dutch tulips in their east flower bed.

PUNCTUATION:

   Punctuate these titles:

2.   A.   (chapter)   Insects
       B.   (magazine) My Backyard
       C.   (magazine article) Super Jaws
       D.   (book)   Come Follow Me
       E.   (nursery rhyme)   Hickory Dickory Dock

PARTS OF SPEECH: PRONOUNS / ADJECTIVES

   Determine if the underlined word serves as an adjective or as a pronoun:

3.   A.   The director gave <u>this</u> direction.
       B.   Do you understand <u>this</u>?

PARTS OF SPEECH: ADJECTIVES / ADVERBS

   Select the correct answer:

4.   The teller does her job _____ (well, good).

SENTENCE COMBINING:

5.   Millie's first answer was five.
       Millie's first answer was incorrect.
       Millie's second answer was right.

CAPITALIZATION:

1. during their hawaiian trip, a polynesian* luau was held at waikiki beach.

    * referring to a place called Polynesia

PUNCTUATION:

2. I think said Marion that your shoe is untied

PARTS OF SPEECH: PREPOSITIONS

Cross out prepositional phrases.   Underline the subject once and the verb/verb phrase twice:

3. Throughout the day, squirrels rushed in and out among the trees.

DIRECT OBJECTS:

Underline the subject once and the verb/verb phrase twice;   label direct object(s):

4. We ate doughnuts and drank juice for breakfast.

SENTENCE COMBINING:

5. Salco Industries is on Porter Avenue.
   Salco makes mirrors.
   These mirrors are for cars.

DAY 178

CAPITALIZATION:

Capitalize these titles:

1.   A.   <u>if there were dreams to sell</u>
          B.   "a million and one wishes"
          C.   "an apple for colliwobble"
          D.   "barry has a fright"
          E.   "the boy who chased after a cow"

PUNCTUATION:

2.   Janices sister left Nashville Tennessee yesterday

BUSINESS LETTER:

Using your own address for the heading, do an inside address:

3.   You are writing to Tatum Company located in San Diego, California, at 12 Mission Bay Drive. The zip code is 92109.

PARTS OF SPEECH: NOUNS

Select nouns:

4.   The back door of the house opens to a patio.

SENTENCE COMBINING:

5.   The street sweeper came today.
        My friend's grandpa drives the sweeper.

CAPITALIZATION:

1.   his uncle gil owns an arabian horse in santa fe, new mexico.

PUNCTUATION:

2.   Hasnt the girls swimming team returned Miss Hart

PARTS OF SPEECH: VERBS

Select the correct verb; underline the verb phrase twice:

3.   The sunbather had _____ (laid, lain) there all day.

SENTENCE TYPES:

Determine the type of sentence:

4.   A.   This is great!
      B.   Why did you go?
      C.   Stay here.
      D.   The charge is ten cents.

SENTENCE COMBINING:

5.   A book is on the floor.
      The book is about birds.
      Please pick it up.

DAY 180

CAPITALIZATION:

Capitalize this letter:

1.   (A)   brak lane
                                          chelsea mi 48118
                                          dec 12 19--

    (B)   my very good friend

    (C)   were looking forward to visiting shelter island
the zoo and a mexican food restaurant

                          (D)   your pal
                          (E)   shelly l jabbel

PUNCTUATION:

2.   Punctuate the above letter.

FRIENDLY LETTERS:

3.   Label the parts of the friendly letter.

PARTS OF SPEECH: PRONOUNS

4.   List the pronouns used as objects.

SENTENCE COMBINING:

5.   Taley's parents went to Ohio.
        Taley stayed with her aunt.

DAY 1: 1. Have, Dr., Mrs., C., Winston, New, York 2. Jill, are you going? 3. a child's balloon 4. <u>Janet</u> <u>sneezed</u> 5. AMV/RA*: The yellow pen is on the table. The pen on the table is yellow.

DAY 2: 1. Their, Elm, Street 2. No, don't go. (!) 3. A. isn't B. they're C. can't 4. question (interrogative) 5. AMV/RA: The black fly is on the ceiling. On the ceiling is a black fly.

DAY 3: 1. The, Fairmont, School, Birk, Lane 2. Wow! I won! 3. <u>band</u> <u>marches</u> 4. A. question (interrogative) B. statement (declarative) 5. AMV/RA: Mark is sick today, and he had to stay home. Mark stayed home because he was sick today.

DAY 4: 1. My, San, Diego, California 2. Tom, can you play? 3. articles 4. <u>dog</u> <u>licks</u> 5. AMV/RA: The green and pink basket is broken. The broken basket is green and pink.

DAY 5: 1. Did, Sandy, Prince, Street 2. Sue, Frank, and Lil were first. 3. <u>chain</u> <u>fell</u> 4. carefully 5. AMV/RA: The telephone rang and Ted answered it. When the telephone rang, Ted answered it.

DAY 6: 1. Last, Sunday, Nancy, Austin, Texas 2. He was born on Oct. 20, 1980. 3. Today 4. I (subject) 5. AMV/RA: Debbie fixed her bike's flat tire. When Debbie's bike had a flat tire, she fixed it.

DAY 7: 1. Last, Christmas, Susan's, Hawaii 2. Mary, have you been to Denver, Colorado? 3. down 4. A. command (imperative) B. statement (declarative) 5. AMV/RA: The dropped dish broke into many pieces. When the dish was dropped, it broke into many pieces.

DAY 8: 1. In, August, Grand, Canyon, Arizona 2. Dear Ben, I'll meet you soon. Your friend, Mickey 3. and, but, or 4. several (several cats) 5. AMV/RA: Joe's mom and dad are dentists. Both Joe's mom and dad are dentists.

DAY 9: 1. Has, Mrs., Jones, Summer, Monkeys 2. Anaheim, California, is the home of Disneyland. 3. this (this picture) 4. <u>horse</u> <u>chews</u> 5. AMV/RA: The roses were blooming, but the daisies were not. Although the roses were blooming, the daisies were not.

*AMV/RA: ANSWERS MAY VARY / REPRESENTATIVE ANSWERS

DAY 10: 1. Was, George, Washington's, Mount, Vernon 2. Marge, Frank, and Miriam left early. 3. Their (Their dad) 4. <u>trees</u> <u>sway</u>* 5. AMV/RA: Jason mailed a letter for his dad. Jason mailed his dad's letter.

*<u>NOTE</u>: Students will eventually be asked to cross out prepositional phrases to simplify identification of subject and verb. You may want to explain the concept and provide them with a list of prepositions.

The prepositional approach to grammar is explained in **EASY GRAMMAR** by Wanda C. Phillips. (See last page.)

DAY 11: 1. Dear, Terry, I, June, Your, Tony 2. Mary is coming at 10:15 A.M. 3. A. shouldn't B. aren't C. he'll D. I'm E. I've F. won't 4. a, an, the 5. AMV/RA: Because the chalkboard was dusty, two students washed it. Two students washed the dusty chalkboard.

DAY 12: 1. The, Dr., Kolb, Saddle, River, New, Jersey 2. Mrs. Tate doesn't have a marker. 3. Cold (cold sandwiches), chocolate (chocolate cake) 4. The <u>bus</u> <del>with flashing lights</del> <u>stopped</u>. 5. AMV/RA: Jane's ten-year-old brother is on the swim team. Jane's brother who is ten years old is on the swim team.

DAY 13: 1. On, Monday, Memorial, Day 2. My aunt's graduation was June 10, 1987. 3. There 4. few (few squirrels), twenty (twenty nuts) 5. AMV/RA: The carriage that was decorated with flowers was pulled by a horse. The carriage pulled by a horse was decorated with flowers.

DAY 14: 1. On, Saturday, Heard, Museum, Palm, Lane 2. Our troop won't leave until 7:00 P.M. 3. big (big balloons), blue (blue balloons) 4. is, am, are, was, were, be, being, been, has, have, had, do, does, did, may, might, must, can, could, shall, should, will, would 5. AMV/RA: Wendy plays first base on a softball team.

DAY 15: 1. The, Smith, East, Ball, Street, Reno, Nevada 2. No, I did not read <u>Blubber</u>. 3. me 4. After the movie, at a diner 5. AMV/RA: When Ken skied for two hours, he fell three times. Ken skied for two hours, and he fell three times.

DAY 16: 1. Matt's, Thunderbird, Bank, Bell, Road 2. One-half of the birds aren't flying. 3. three children's puppy 4. I (subject - Bill and I) 5. AMV/RA: John's suitcase is packed, and he's leaving for vacation tonight. Because John is leaving for vacation tonight, his suitcase is packed.

DAY 17: 1. Was, Virginia, United, States, America 2. A. <u>Corduroy</u> B. "The Balloon" 3. this (this pencil), that (that pen) 4. A. statement (declarative) B. question (interrogative) 5. AMV/RA: David will repair the broken television after school. The television is broken, but David will repair it after school.

DAY 18: 1. Was, Cortes, Spaniard, Mexico 2. A. "Holiday" B. "Tale of a Tail" 3. blue (blue water), cool (cool water), striped (striped fish) 4. I (subject = Barb and I) 5. AMV/RA: The children wore shorts, tops, and sandals. Shorts, sandals, and tops were worn by the children.

DAY 19: 1. A. <u>The Cat in the Hat</u> B. "Goldilocks and the Three Bears" 2. Bob's mother flew to St. Augustine, Florida. 3. A. command (imperative) B. question (interrogative) 4. A. heading B. greeting C. message (body) D. closing E. signature 5. AMV/RA: A deer ate grass in a wide green meadow.

DAY 20: 1. The, United, Bank, Building, Phoenix, Arizona 2. Hasn't Joel read <u>Little Deer</u> to you? 3. A. question (interrogative) B. exclamation (exclamatory) 4. helping (auxiliary) 5. AMV/RA: A Utah teacher spoke about Indian life. A teacher from Utah spoke about Indian life.

DAY 21: 1. Does, Steve, Sax, Los, Angeles, Dodgers 2. Yes, Tammy's dog had puppies. 3. run; <u>had run</u> 4. A. holidays B. studies C. dishes* D. calves 5. AMV/RA: The toddlers are playing with yellow and red toy cars. The toddlers are playing with toy cars that are yellow and red.

*Note: It is suggested that students **memorize** this rule: Nouns ending in **<u>s</u>, <u>sh</u>, <u>ch</u>, <u>x</u>, and <u>z</u>** add **<u>es</u>** to form the plural.

DAY 22: 1. Karen, I, The, Tale, Peter, Rabbit, Beatrix, Potter 2. Doesn't your uncle live in Orlando, Florida? 3.

<u>MY STREET ADDRESS</u>
<u>CITY, STATE ZIP</u>
<u>TODAY'S DATE</u>

Dear Mrs. Crane,

4. These (These rods), that (that net) 5. AMV/RA: The eagle perches on a dead tree limb. The eagle perches on a dead limb of a tree.

DAY 23: 1. Is, Penn, State, University, Nittany, Mountains 2. Cindy said, "Today is Tuesday." 3. me (me = object of the preposition) 4. fast, carefully 5. AMV/RA: A basket of bright yellow flowers is hanging on her patio. On the patio is hanging a basket of bright yellow flowers.

DAY 24: 1. A, Fann, Company 2. Dear Vivian, How's the summer going for you? A friend always, Candy 3. early, late 4. A. exclamation (exclamatory) B. command (imperative) 5. AMV/RA: In autumn, the trees were dropping their leaves. Because it was autumn, the trees were dropping their leaves.

DAY 25: 1. On, Valentine's, Day, Chante, Chocolate, Store 2. Linda, let's go swimming and play baseball. 3. its (its tail) 4. A. friend B. Elizabeth C. Iowa D. November E. mountain F. Monday 5. AMV/RA: Lily likes to ski, sled, and ice skate. Lily not only enjoys skiing and sledding, but she also likes ice skating.

DAY 26: 1.   I.   Desert animals
              A. Rattlesnakes
              B. Turtles
2. Our new address is 12 Link Drive, Biglerville, Pennsylvania 17307. 3. ~~In the afternoon~~ <u>Grandma</u> <u>was reading</u> ~~in her room~~. 4. chosen; <u>have chosen</u> 5. AMV/RA: The red rose that was taken out of water wilted. Because the red rose was taken out of water, it wilted.

DAY 27: 1. The, Mrs., Blanch, America, Beautiful 2. Was the Declaration of Independence signed July 4, 1776? 3. Jimmy's penny 4. here, there, anywhere 5. AMV/RA: The black and white butterfly is sitting on a tiny daisy. On a tiny daisy sits a black and white butterfly.

DAY 28: 1. A. <u>Monkey Tales</u> B. "The Brave Knight" C. "Hop to It" 2. A. Ave. B. gal. C. Mr. D. ft. E. in. F. St. 3. first (first class), thirty (thirty children) 4. gone; <u>must have gone</u> 5. AMV/RA: The cold water in the glass is for drinking. The cold drinking water is in a glass.

DAY 29: 1. Carlos, Gumdrop, Easter 2. A. Dr. B. c. C. lb. D. Co. E. Dr. F. Ln. 3. A. oxen B. mice C. classes D. buses 4. ~~During the storm~~, the <u>waves</u> <u>were rocking</u> the boat ~~at sea~~. 5. AMV/RA: When Todd rode his bike to Ted's house, they played chess. After Todd rode his bike to Ted's house, they played chess.

DAY 30: 1. Have, Little, House, Prairie, Mesa, Library 2. "Are we leaving at 1:15 P.M. today?" asked Cheri. 3. me (direct object) 4. very (to what extent tired), quite (to what extent happy) 5. AMV/RA: Dad tripped over a toy that was lying on the floor. Dad tripped over the toy lying on the floor.

DAY 31: 1. Last, Niagara, Falls, New, York 2. No, the answer isn't twenty-two. 3. given; <u>should have given</u> 4. Laura's book 5. AMV/RA: The dentist examined Fay's teeth, and she had no cavities. When the dentist examined Fay's teeth, she had no cavities.

DAY 32: 1. A. "Jack and the Beanstalk" B. "All About America" C. <u>Gumdrop Has a Birthday</u> 2. Yes, her nephew lives in Tacoma, Washington, in the summer. 3. driven; <u>had driven</u> 4. The scuba <u>diver</u> <u>arrived</u> ~~in a yellow car~~. 5. AMV/RA: A soft gray kitten crawled onto Tom's lap. Onto Tom's lap crawled a soft gray kitten.

DAY 33: 1. In, Sears, German 2. 34 Lake Avenue / Tucson, Arizona 85705 / January 23, 19--/ 3. so (to what extent hungry), not 4. she (subject = shopper and she) 5. AMV/RA: The girls had fun washing the car. The girls who washed the car had fun.

DAY 34: 1. In, Sleeps, Where, Till 2. Paula asked, "Is John ready?" 3. Suddenly (when), hard (how) 4. YOUR FIRST AND LAST NAME / YOUR STREET ADDRESS / CITY, STATE ZIP 5. AMV/RA: Josh went to a scary movie about monsters. Josh went to a monster movie that was scary.

DAY 35: 1. Did, Japanese, Ohio, River 2. 2 Peat Street / Plano, Texas 75023 / October 21, 19-- / Gorm Industries / 122 North 73rd Avenue / Tulsa, Oklahoma 74145/ Dear Sir: 3. has (magazine has) 4. Darin and I 5. AMV/RA: The cheering fans watched a baseball game. The fans cheered as they watched a baseball game.

DAY 36: 1. Recently, Dr., Polk, Shea, Medical, Building 2. Randy, may I read, swim, or hike today? 3. A. statement (declarative) B. question (interrogative) 4. rougher (comparing two items) 5. AMV/RA: An ant carried a piece of bread as it crawled across the sidewalk.

DAY 37: 1. A, French, Playful, Pet, Palace 2. No, we won't be there by 2:30 P.M. 3. most colorful (comparing three) 4. Some ~~of the sheep~~ were moved ~~to a new field~~. 5. AMV/RA: A carnival to raise money for the fire department will be held soon. Soon, the fire department will hold a fund-raising carnival.

DAY 38: 1. A, Chinese, Birk, August 2. Will you be in Topeka, Kansas, next week, Marvin? 3. A. Gulf of Mexico B. river C. lake D. Lake Erie E. Mississippi River F. street 4. well (adverb telling how) 5. AMV/RA: When the boys raced, Dave won. Dave won the boys' race.

DAY 39: 1. Have, Statue, Liberty, New, York, City 2. Jerry exclaimed, "Jump on!" 3. A. don't B. I'll C. they're D. hasn't E. I've F. she'll 4. A. question (interrogative) B. command (imperative) 5. AMV/RA: The small child who had an ear infection cried. Because the small child had an ear infection, he cried.

DAY 40: 1. One, England, Queen, Victoria 2. I. Famous airplanes/ A. Spirit of St. Louis / B. Spruce Goose / II. Famous ships 3. Never (when), outside (where) 4. too 5. AMV/RA: Lois read a book containing one hundred pages. Lois read a book that contained one hundred pages.

DAY 41: 1. Did, Reverend, Sells, St., James, Lutheran, Church 2. Millie asked, "When is the party?" 3. gone 4. A. pens B. wishes C. monkeys D. deer E. envelopes 5. AMV/RA: The puppy who is in the backyard is chasing a ball. The puppy in the backyard is chasing a ball.

DAY 42: 1. When, A., T., Arkin, Chicago's 2. Joyce laughed loudly, but her sister cried. 3. A. flashes B. stories C. children D. bays E. films 4. A. command (imperative) B. exclamation (exclamatory) C. statement (declarative) 5. AMV/RA: The child sneezed, coughed, and took a tissue from the box. The sneezing child also coughed and took a tissue from the box.

DAY 43: 1. The, The, Midnight, Ride, Paul, Revere, Listen 2. I. Parts of speech / A. Nouns / B. Pronouns / II. Word parts / A. Prefixes / B. Suffixes 3. Their 4. Tom and Nancy's house 5. AMV/RA: The red car has a flat tire. The car painted red has a flat tire.

DAY 44: 1. A, Gleeful, Gardener's, Club, Ingle, Inn 2. "Who is your leader?" asked Carl. 3. now, later 4. few (few boys), one (one friend) 5. AMV/RA: Mary writes letters to her aunt and to her cousin. Mary writes letters both to her aunt and to her cousin.

DAY 45: 1. Dear, Mr., Flan, Your, From, Funny, Bear, Sincerely, Meg, Lewis 2. "I like the ice cream," said the clown. 3. Some (Some flowers), two (two gardens) 4. storm had blown 5. AMV/RA: Because the candy bar was left in the sun, it melted. The melted candy bar had been left in the sun.

DAY 46: 1. Two, Chinese, Empire, State, Building 2. They ate pizza, drank cola, and played ball. 3. two girls' lamb 4. comes 5. AMV/RA: Tracey couldn't find her sneakers because they were under her bed. Tracey couldn't find her sneakers that were under her bed.

DAY 47: 1. Has, C., T., Smith, Yosemite, National, Park 2. The R. J. Lincoln Co. opened last Thursday, Nov. 29. 3. Dave and I will fish 4. A. command (imperative) B. exclamation (exclamatory) C. question (interrogative) 5. AMV/RA: My Uncle Phil teaches art at a junior high.

DAY 48: 1. Many, Americans, Veterans', Day 2. "I'd like to see that play," Sharon said. 3. librarian's books 4. quietly 5. AMV/RA: A play that began today is being performed at Dikson School. A play at Dikson School began today.

DAY 49: 1. Their, Glenrok, Art, Museum, Friday 2. His brother was born on Feb. 6, 1984, in a local hospital. 3. These (These shoes), that (that dress) 4. faster 5. AMV/RA: When Rob threw the ball, Sally caught it. Rob threw the ball, and Sally caught it.

DAY 50: 1. Will, The, Story, Old, King, Cole 2. A. <u>Moby Dick</u> B. "Millie" C. "If" D. <u>Teen</u> 3. **do**n't 4. A. boxes B. brushes C. rays D. mice E. secretaries 5. AMV/RA: Susan collects stickers, stamps, and shells. Susan not only collects stickers, but she also collects stamps and shells.

DAY 51: 1. Is, Statue, Liberty, New, York, City, Liberty, Island 2. Amy's report isn't finished yet. 3. B. Truly yours, 4. me (direct object) 5. AMV/RA: Because Sally's lock was broken, she bought a new one. When Sally's lock broke, she bought a new one.

DAY 52: 1. Little, Jonathon, The, Sesame, Street, Treasury 2. Wow! I've jumped nearly four feet, Mrs. Dill. 3. A. proper B. common C. common D. proper E. common 4. rings 5. AMV/RA: We watched television and ate popcorn. While we watched television, we ate popcorn.

DAY 53: 1. Last, Mrs., Kirk's, Elton, Street 2. June's pen won't work on this three-ply paper. 3. their 4. ~~At dawn~~ some <u>swans</u> <u>swam</u> ~~on a pond~~. 5. AMV/RA: The artist drew a picture of a clown. The man drawing a clown picture is an artist.

DAY 54: 1. 333 Strom Street / Shippensburg, PA 17257 / April 22, 19-- / Dear Larry, 2. Bobbi said, "Yes, I am ready." 3. A white furry <u>bunny</u> <u>hopped</u> ~~into our garden~~. 4. A. Xerox Corporation B. Mummy Mountain C. newspaper D. Fido E. springer spaniel 5. AMV/RA: The delicious dessert was apple pie. The apple pie for dessert was delicious.

DAY 55: 1. Have, I, Your, Big, Backyard 2. Dad, where's Sen. Blatz going? 3. some girls' candy bar 4. in the middle, of the room, from China 5. AMV/RA: The fraction test was difficult. The test about fractions was difficult.

DAY 56: 1. In, July, South, Mountain, Fair 2. The story entitled "Pinocchio" isn't sad. 3. Eagerly, hard 4. a, an, the 5. AMV/RA: Jill went ice skating, but her brother went sledding. Although Jill went ice skating, her brother went sledding.

DAY 57: 1. The, R., O., Dott, Co., East, Elm, Lane, Lubbock, Texas 2. "I want a sandwich," remarked Brett. 3. Those (Those glasses) 4. Now, then 5. AMV/RA: The owl sat in a tree and hooted. Sitting in the tree, the owl hooted.*

*NOTE: This is a more difficult sentence combining. However, the concept of beginning with a participial phrase can be taught easily.

DAY 58: 1. The, Taking, Care, Your, Pet 2. Mr. Jones thinks that the children's playground needs grass. 3. up, down 4. <u>YOUR FIRST AND LAST NAME / YOUR STREET ADDRESS / CITY, STATE   ZIP</u> 5. AMV/RA: Because Gloria was shouting for her brother, she became hoarse. Shouting for her brother, Gloria became hoarse.

DAY 59: 1. When, Sam, United, States, Marine, Corps 2. They're arriving late, and I'll pick them up at the airport. 3. taller (comparing two) 4. and, but, or 5. AMV/RA: Alice's message was written in ink and in letter form. The letter written in ink was a message from Alice.

DAY 60: 1. Have, Mr., Lott, Dr., Jones, Top, Seed, Club 2. Tom's uncle was born Jan. 30, 1950, in Ohio. 3. Tomorrow, early 4. ~~In the morning~~ Mom and <u>Dad</u> <u>are</u> <u>driving</u> ~~to Montana.~~ 5. AMV/RA: The bumpy dirt road has many loose stones. The dirt road with many loose stones is bumpy.

DAY 61: 1. The, Thomas, A., Edison 2. George, have you been to St. Louis, Missouri, in the winter? 3. A. haven't B. you're C. he'll D. they've E. I'm 4. two (two friends), some (some candy) 5. AMV/RA: The concert was cancelled because the singer was sick. The singer was sick, and the concert was cancelled.

DAY 62: 1. Their, Alaskan, Blue, Moose, Lodge 2. Carrie exclaimed, "Look at that boat!" 3. A. boys B. crashes C. buzzes D. fields E. babies 4. A. question (interrogative) B. statement (declarative) C. command (imperative) 5. AMV/RA: While Mom made sandwiches, Dad made a salad for lunch. For lunch, Mom made the sandwiches, and Dad made a salad.

DAY 63: 1. My, I, White, Cliff, Road 2. Lori, stand up, and I'll measure you. 3. I (subject = Jill and I) 4. blue (blue shirt), red (red skirt) 5. AMV/RA: Orange juice was served first, and milk was served later. Milk was served after orange juice.

DAY 64: 1. The, Swartz, Dade, County, Florida 2. 52 Elm Ln.* / Gettysburg, PA 17325 / May 8, 19-- / Dear Sam, 3. eaten; <u>had eaten</u> 4. Chris's fork 5. AMV/RA: Nancy runs faster than Rudy. Although Rudy runs fast, Nancy runs faster.

*NOTE: In formal writing, no abbreviations are acceptable. However, as a practice in punctuation, abbreviations have been added here.

DAY 65: 1. Was, Yankee, Stadium, New, York 2. Wow! We did it, Sean! 3. They, their 4. A. couldn't B. it's C. I'm D. can't E. won't 5. AMV/RA: Fifteen friends attended Randy's birthday party. Randy had a birthday party, and fifteen friends came.

DAY 66: 1. A, Chinese, Ming's, Golden, Dragon, Thursday 2. Is Rebecca's horse, Mr. Pratt, ready to ride? 3. is, am, are, was, were, be, being, been, do, does, did, has, have, had, may, might, must, shall, should, could, can, will, would 4. Their (their uncle) 5. AMV/RA: The day was cold, sunny, and windy. Although the day was sunny, it was windy and cold.

DAY 67: 1. Did, Fourth, July, Independence, Day 2. One-third of Marge's doll collection is from London, England. 3. We 4. slowly, carefully 5. AMV/RA: Because Cameron has spilled lemonade, the floor is wet. Cameron has spilled lemonade, and the floor is wet.

DAY 68: 1. At, Dobson, Theater, The, King, I 2. A. <u>Tex</u> B. "Cat and the Underworld" C. <u>Ranger Rick</u> 3. sings (<u>clown sings</u>) 4. A. exclamation (exclamatory) B. command (imperative) C. statement (declarative) 5. AMV/RA: Her brown curly hair needs to be combed.

DAY 69: 1. His, February, Presidents', Day 2. Mom's exercise class will meet Friday at 2 P.M. 3. A. heading B. greeting (salutation) C. message (body) D. closing E. signature 4. helping verb(s) 5. AMV/RA: We are going to the state fair next week. We will be attending next week's state fair.

DAY 70: 1. On, Monday, Mayor, Tilson, American, Airlines, Salem, Oregon 2. I'm wondering if you've read <u>Blubber</u>. 3. is, am, are, was, were, be, being, been, do, does, did, has, have, had, may, might, must, shall, should, will, would, can, could 4. anything 5. AMV/RA: Mrs. Patts is a pilot who owns an airplane. Mrs. Patts, a pilot, owns an airplane.*

*NOTE: This is a good place to review the concept of appositives.

DAY 71: 1. Has, Senator, R., C., Cline, Congress 2. Sally asked, "Where's Mike's new boat?" 3. known; <u>should have known</u> 4. him 5. AMV/RA: While lying on the floor, the boys watched television and ate popcorn. The boys who were lying on the floor, ate popcorn, and watched television.

DAY 72: 1. When, Aunt, Bea, Elton, Golden, Express 2. No, I won't go, and Tami doesn't want to go either. (!) 3. rather (rather old), very (very odd)

NOTE: It is suggested that students learn the 7 adverbs commonly used to tell <u>to what extent</u>: **not, so, too, very, rather, quite,** and **somewhat.**

4. sit 5. AMV/RA: Crater Lake in Oregon is very deep. Oregon's Crater Lake is very deep.

DAY 73: 1. Did, Dad, Anaheim, Hilton, Hotel, Disneyland 2. Joy asked, "Have you read <u>The Staircase</u>?" 3. I 4. those (those kittens) 5. AMV/RA: I bought daisies from a flower shop that just opened last week. That flower shop just opened last week, and I bought some daisies.

DAY 74: 1. On, Veteran's, Day, Culver, Avenue, Loe, Park 2. The men's club listened to a speech entitled "Time Wasters." 3. and, but, or 4. <u>Many</u> ~~of the flowers~~ <u>had</u> already <u>bloomed</u>. 5. AMV/RA: The pink ceramic vase was filled with straw. The vase filled with straw was a pink ceramic one.

DAY 75: 1. For, Canadian, Max's, Deli 2. Kim said, "My brother is twenty-one years old." 3. A. common B. proper C. proper D. proper E. common 4. few (few joggers), six (six miles) 5. AMV/RA: Joanie and her sister went ice skating on Bardton Pond. Joanie and her sister went to Bardton Pond to ice skate.

DAY 76: 1. Last, China, Buddhistic 2. The boys' restroom and the locker room won't be open. 3. more carefully 4. a, an, the 5. AMV/RA: Jim's lunch consisting of a sandwich and cookies is in the refrigerator. In the refrigerator is Jim's lunch, a sandwich and cookies.

DAY 77: 1. A, Swiss, Kennedy, Airport, New, York 2. At 10:00 A.M. on Saturday, May 12, 1965, the couple met. 3. ridden; <u>has ridden</u> 4. A. question (interrogative) B. statement (declarative) C. command (imperative) 5. AMV/RA: This new blue watch was given to Barbara as a graduation gift. For graduation, Barbara was given a new blue watch.

DAY 78: 1. Our, Mayor, Dobbs, Terrace, Guest, House 2. Joe read <u>Where the Red Fern Grows</u>, and he wrote a report. 3. <u>Marta</u>, <u>Tina</u>, and <u>Bob</u> <u>will be rehearsing</u> ~~in an hour~~. 4. not, so, very, quite, rather, too, somewhat 5. AMV/RA: Mom and Dad caught five fish at a lake. When Mom and Dad went fishing at a lake, they caught five fish.

DAY 79: 1. During, Labor, Day, Rev., Little's 2. Mark asked, "Where's the three-pronged fork?" 3. Some (Some trees), seven (seven planters) 4. A. moose B. friends C. gulfs D. fences E. churches 5. AMV/RA: When the bike race began, I fell off my bike and skinned my knee.

DAY 80: 1. Did, Uncle, Bill, Hotel, Herald, Los, Angeles, Convention, Center 2. The librarian read to us, gave us a quiz, and graded the papers. 3. day (throughout the day), roof (on the roof) 4. STUDENT'S STREET ADDRESS / CITY, STATE ZIP / TODAY'S DATE 5. AMV/RA: During the class's free time, two girls played dominoes, and three boys read. While two girls played dominoes, three boys read during the class's free time.

DAY 81: 1. The, We, Professor, Gibb 2. A. "Arise and Shine" B. <u>Roll of Thunder, Hear My Cry</u> C. "Verbs" D. "On a Rainy Day" 3. this, that, those, these 4. A. pies B. flashes C. derbies D. pays E. oxen 5. AMV/RA: His blue tennis shoes are lying in the corner of the room.

DAY 82: 1. The, German, San, Francisco, Korean, War 2. Paul, won't you take this self-propelling object to the park? 3. five ladies' business 4. Martha's <u>uncle</u> and her <u>cousin</u> <u>will be</u> in that race. 5. AMV/RA: Tom's aunt, Susan Bothe, is a teacher. Susan Bothe is Tom's aunt, and she is a teacher.

DAY 83: 1. The, Arbor, Day, Fimm, Park 2. Sue asked, "How's your grandmother feeling, Julie?" 3. A. present tense B. past tense 4. AMV/RA: Yours truly, / Student Name / , Love, / Student Name 5. AMV/RA: The palomino is named Colonel. The horse, a palomino, is named Colonel.

DAY 84: 1. Has, Liberty, Bell, Independence, Hall 2. Sally's flight leaves on Friday, June 8th, at 12:30 A.M. 3. Ted and Jay's flag 4. she 5. AMV/RA: The green wagon has black tires and a new handle. The wagon with green paint has a new handle and black tires.

DAY 85: 1. This, Ruth 2. Sarah's first teacher was Miss Dow. 3. is, am, are, was, were, be, being, been 4. its (its paws) 5. AMV/RA: Because it rained all day, the children had to stay inside. The children had to remain inside when it rained all day.

DAY 86: 1. On, Mothers', Day, Mom, Mexican 2. "Don't go," pleaded Peter. 3. a, an, the 4. Sue and James's pancakes 5. AMV/RA: One monkey was sitting on a tree limb while another monkey was swinging on a rope. One monkey was sitting on a tree limb, and another monkey was swinging on a rope.

DAY 87: 1. A. "A Bicycle Built for Two" B. <u>Days of Our Lives</u> C. <u>The Night Before Christmas</u> D. <u>To Sir, with Love</u> 2. Jan's sister-in-law is from Toledo, Ohio. 3. hardest 4. A. concrete B. abstract C. abstract D. concrete 5. AMV/RA: An invitation to Gail and Gabe's wedding arrived in the mail. Because Gail and Gabe will marry, an invitation to their wedding arrived in the mail.

DAY 88: 1. When, Bill, I, Bree, Mall, Chris's, Craft, Cabin 2. Lyle asked, "Isn't your dad coming at 3:30 P.M. for you?" 3. two babies' ball 4. A. statement (declarative) B. question (interrogative) C. exclamation (exclamatory) D. command (imperative) 5. AMV/RA: Jill gave the clerk a dollar for the candy bar, and the clerk returned the change. When Jill gave the clerk a dollar for a candy bar, she was given change.

DAY 89: 1. A, Memorial, Day, World, War 2. In <u>Reader's Digest</u>* there is an article entitled "Young America." 3. those (those shoes) 4. children's bugs 5. AMV/RA: Jean read a newspaper article that stated a circus would soon be coming to town. Reading an article in the newspaper, Jean learned that a circus would soon be coming to town.

* A comma is also acceptable.

DAY 90: 1. In, November, U., S., House, Representatives 2. Cindy's essay entitled "America's Story" isn't finished. 3. Friday, Saturday 4. This (This award), that (that student) 5. AMV/RA: The black sky seemed to predict a storm. Because the sky was black, it looked like a storm was coming.

DAY 91: 1. The, Shoshone, Indian, Sacajawea 2. Teri, haven't you found a book, a pen, or a notebook? 3. her (antecedent = girl) 4. The <u>director</u> and her <u>crew</u> <u>had</u> <u>filmed</u> the movie ~~at night~~. 5. AMV/RA: Cody made a noodle necklace in nursery school. Cody's noodle necklace was made in nursery school.

DAY 92: 1. We, Swedish, Elegante, Cafe, Elm, Street 2. A. <u>Insights</u> B. "If" C. <u>Chicago Tribune</u> D. "Katie" 3. A. 1. give, gives 2. gave B. 1. walk, walks 2. walked 4. up, where 5. AMV/RA: At the zoo, we saw a mother gorilla with her baby.

DAY 93: 1. For, Thanksgiving, Mississippi 2. Marty, where's the <u>TV Guide</u>? 3. A. faces B. stories C. wishes D. pianos E. geese 4. A. sang B. yelled (NOTE: This may be a good time to review regular and irregular verb differences.) 5. AMV/RA: The check on the table is for your lunch. Your lunch check is on the table.

DAY 94: 1. Every, Christmas, Eve, Gray, Baptist 2. The Rev. R. Dobbs spoke about life in 1215 B.C. 3. interjection 4. A. given B. walked 5. AMV/RA: Because the glue stick was on the floor, Jim picked it up. Jim picked up the glue stick from the floor.

DAY 95: 1. Did, Mayor, Link, French, Atlantic, Ocean 2. I. Important holidays / A. Memorial Day / B. Armistice Day / II. Special days / A. April Fool's Day / B. Ground Hog's Day 3. not, so, very, too, quite, rather, somewhat 4. ~~At our picnic in the spring,~~ <u>Jenny</u> and her <u>dad</u> <u>played</u> ball. 5. AMV/RA: Milly and Cal are horseback riding in the forest. Milly and Cal rode their horses into the forest.

DAY 96: 1. Has, William, Perry, Chicago, Bears 2. Ted, two-thirds of the peaches won't be sold. 3. the, a, an 4. I (subject = Ryan and I) 5. AMV/RA: The six tomato plants that Micah planted grew large and produced many tomatoes. Micah's six tomato plants grew large and produced many tomatoes.

DAY 97:   1. Next, July, Dallas, Museum, Art, Texas 2. "This week we expect twenty-one inches of snow," said the lady. 3. broken; <u>must have broken</u> 4. One (One artist), many (many paintings) 5. AMV/RA: Sheri filled the empty stapler. When the stapler was empty, Sheri filled it.

DAY 98:   1. In, Senator, Lee, Columbia, South, America
2.

> 2 Doe Street
> Scottsdale, Arizona   85254
> March 7, 19--

> Dear Tom,
>   How are you doing? We'll see you in a few months.
>   Your friend,
>   Matt

3. A. heading B. greeting (salutation) C. message (body) D. closing E. signature
4. is, am, are, was, were, be, being, been, has, have, had, do, does, did, may, must, might, shall, should, will, would, can, could 5. AMV/RA: The chocolate cake for Joe's birthday is in the oven. Joe's chocolate birthday cake is in the oven.

DAY 99:   1. H., B., Hicks, Company, Indian, Ohio 2. At 9:00 P.M. on Friday, July 4th, there will be fireworks. 3. <u>Some</u> ~~of the dogs~~ <u>stayed</u> ~~near their masters during the show.~~ 4. A. abstract B. abstract C. concrete D. concrete E. abstract 5. AMV/RA: Because Richard has an ear infection, his mother put drops in his ear. To help Richard's infected ear, his mother put drops in it.

DAY 100:   1. His, American, University, Iowa 2. Your report, Lisa, is due Friday, Sept. 8, at noon. 3. A. they've B. doesn't C. I'll D. won't E. she's F. isn't G. can't H. she'd 4. me (object of the preposition = you and me) 5. AMV/RA: The children bought their dad a book for Fathers' Day. For a Fathers' Day gift, the children bought their dad a book.

DAY 101:   1. In, The, Legend, Sleepy, Hollow 2. "You're the greatest," said the coach, "so try your best." 3. A. run(s), ran, (has/have/had) run B. create(s), created, (has/have/had) created C. do(es), did, (has/have/had) done 4. ~~During the morning~~, the <u>dancers</u> <u>practiced</u> ~~outside the theater.~~ 5. AMV/RA: Peggy and Darrell are trying quickly to remove the furniture polish that has been spilled on the carpeting. Because furniture polish has been spilled on the carpeting, Peggy and Darrell are quickly trying to remove it.

DAY 102:   1. Last, A, Trip, My, Family, English 2. Lynn Batt / 12 Trow St. / Plano, Texas 75074 / Mr. and Mrs. Bob L. Suite / P. O. Box 34 / Peoria, Arizona   85345 3. six (six children), some (some puddles) 4. Yesterday, later 5. AMV/RA: Because the street lights are on, the children must come in.

DAY 103: 1. The, R., R., Bowker, Co., Seventeenth, Street, New, York 2. A. "Your Muscles" B. <u>Benji</u> C. <u>Los Angeles Times</u> D. "Boating" 3. ~~In the afternoon~~, the <u>girl</u> and her <u>dog</u> <u>ran</u>. 4. A. command (imperative) B. statement (declarative) C. exclamation (exclamatory) 5. AMV/RA: The actress who played the part of Juliet is my sister. My sister is an actress who played the part of Juliet.

DAY 104: 1. The, Dons, Club, Sierra, Elementary, School 2. Jack said, "There's that old-fashioned trolley." 3. AMV/RA: A. Littlestown B. John Smith C. Verde Valley Church D. Kentucky E. India F. AT&T 4. A. laugh(s), laughed, (has/have/had) laughed B. speak(s), spoke, (has/have/had) spoken 5. AMV/RA: The cat purred, meowed, and darted across the street. After purring, the cat meowed and darted across the street.

DAY 105: 1. For, Kim, Tales, Fourth, Grade, Nothing
2.
                                                    31 Core Dr.
                                                    Birmingham, Alabama 35223
                                                    Sept. 27, 19--

   Dear Ted,
       I'll be home for Thanksgiving because I'm paying half-fare.
                                                    Sincerely,
                                                    Bart

3. interjection 4. taller 5. AMV/RA: Jan is our school's fastest runner, and she is on the track team. Jan, who is our school's fastest runner, is on the track team.

DAY 106: 1. When, Professor, Jamit, Arctic, Ocean 2. Yeah! We're on our way to Richmond, Virginia, for a week! 3. any 4. A. deer B. ladies C. bugs D. geese E. plants F. bunches 5. AMV/RA: The green hay wagon is being pulled by two horses. A hay wagon that is green is being pulled by two horses.

DAY 107: 1. The, Rocky, Mountains, West 2. A. "McDingle McSquire" B. <u>Fred the Frog</u> C. "The Flying Dwarf" D. "Sleep" 3. <u>Jay</u> <u>had hit</u> the ball ~~to first base~~. 4. <u>s</u>, <u>sh</u>, <u>ch</u>, <u>x</u>, <u>z</u> 5. AMV/RA: Diana dropped a glass, but it did not break. The glass that Diana dropped did not break.

DAY 108: 1. The, Belville, Fire, Department, Labor, Day 2. Larry exclaimed, "Yeah! We're going in one-half hour!" 3. thrown; <u>must have thrown</u> 4. my, mine, his, her, hers, its, your, yours, our, ours, their, whose 5. AMV/RA: The yellow wooden chair is broken. The yellow chair made of wood is broken.

DAY 109: 1. Did, Mother, Pocahontas 2. The Rev. Capp finished his sermon, and the people departed. 3. seen; <u>could have seen</u> 4. YOUR FIRST AND LAST NAME / YOUR STREET ADDRESS / CITY, STATE ZIP 5. AMV/RA: Although twenty stories were entered in the contest, Paula's won.

DAY 110: 1. The, Shinto, Japan 2. Stephanie's dad lives at 23 Cobb Lane, Memphis, Tennessee. 3. brought; <u>should have brought</u> 4. and, but, or 5. AMV/RA: Although the dance is tonight, Joanna is going to a friend's house. Joanna is not going to tonight's dance; she is going to a friend's house.

DAY 111: 1. A. <u>The Door in the Way</u> B. <u>Go Jump in the Pool</u> C. <u>Our Roommate Is Missing</u> 2. Susan, your dog is cute, friendly, and frisky. 3. Mother's cups 4. A. statement (declarative) B. command (imperative) C. exclamation (exclamatory) 5. AMV/RA: The chef made soup, a pie, and potato salad.

DAY 112: 1. Has, Senator, Jim, Fann, Kiwanis, Club 2. A. <u>What Spot?</u> B. "The Penguin" C. "Pirate" D. <u>Jack and Jill</u> 3. two girls' dog 4. third (third pitch), two (two runners) 5. AMV/RA: The silver tray that Grandma has given to Judy has tarnished. The tarnished, silver tray was given to Judy by Grandma.

DAY 113: 1. Last, Brenda, They, Golden, Gate, Bridge 2. On Thurs., December 12th, we will arrive in Lansing, Michigan. 3. <u>Jan finished</u> her speech and <u>sat</u> down ~~behind the podium~~. 4. A. statement (declarative) B. command (imperative) C. question (interrogative) 5. AMV/RA: After the plant dropped its leaves, new ones appeared. New leaves appeared after the old ones had dropped from the plant.

DAY 114: 1. In, Washington, D., C., Alex, Jefferson, Memorial 2. Yes, I'm going to Miami, Florida, in the morning. 3. it's (it's = it is) 4. slowly (adverb telling <u>how</u>) 5. AMV/RA: Mark's dental office is in Vitter Square. Mark is a dentist whose office is in Vitter Square.

DAY 115: 1. In, February, St., Valentine's, Kolb, Lodge 2. On December 7, 1941, there was an attack on Pearl Harbor, Hawaii. 3. any 4. A. railroad B. Reading Railroad C. teacher D. dog E. Fido F. Berwick School 5. AMV/RA: The Indian told a legend about the tribe's first warrior. The legend told by the Indian concerned the tribe's first warrior.

DAY 116: 1. A, Calvary, Methodist, Church, Idaho 2. Shirley remarked, "By the way, I'll take the early bus." 3. your 4. they're 5. AMV/RA: The children played checkers, and Matt was the winner. When the children played checkers, Matt was the winner.

DAY 117: 1. Is, Pike's Peak, Colorado, Springs, Colorado 2. Kent, isn't the answer twenty-four and three-fifths? 3. my, his, her, your, our, their 4. ~~From July until August,~~ the <u>troop</u> <u>will camp</u> out. 5. AMV/RA: During their picnic in the forest, they picked up pine cones. When they picnicked* in the forest, they picked up pine cones.

*NOTE: When a vowel begins a suffix, <u>k</u> is added to <u>picnic</u>.

DAY 118: 1. My, Aunt, Julie, Yellowstone, National, Park 2. Did you, Cindy, see the sleek, new boats? 3. I (subject = Sheila and I) 4. A (A child), happy (happy child), laughing (laughing child), funny (funny songs) 5. AMV/RA: The girl is water-skiing for the first time. This is the girl's first attempt at water-skiing.

DAY 119: 1. In, President, Kennedy, Civil, War 2. The ladies' club meets at 12 Elm St., Bangor, Maine, on Mondays. 3. A. pronoun B. adjective (that hat) 4. A brown <u>mouse</u> <u>ran</u> ~~through the hallway~~ and <u>sneezed</u>. 5. AMV/RA: Their father, who is a policeman, works the night shift. Their father, a policeman, works the night shift.

DAY 120: 1. Has, Jane's, American, Airlines 2. He's usually calm, cool, and collected. 3. Often (when), there (where) 4. noon (By noon), Friday (on Friday), mail (in the mail) 5. AMV/RA: When Charles went to the grocery store, he bought popsicles. Charles bought popsicles at the grocery store.

DAY 121: 1. Is, Jacob, Lawrence's, The, Migration, Negro 2. Yes, they'll spend the night, and we'll serve breakfast. 3. cars, raceway, lap 4. A. statement (declarative) B. exclamation (exclamatory) C. question (interrogative) D. command (imperative) 5. AMV/RA: Led by the mayor, a children's band marched down Main Street. The children's band that marched down Main Street was led by the mayor.

DAY 122: 1. 77 Lark Drive / Lancaster, Kentucky 40446 / January 13, 19-- / My favorite cousin, 2. Your name appeared on the list, in fact, as Jacobs, Ken C. 3. easily (adverb telling <u>how</u>) 4. not, so, very, too, quite, rather, somewhat 5. AMV/RA: The family sold an old bike for twenty dollars at a garage sale. The family had a garage sale and sold an old bike for twenty dollars.

DAY 123: 1. Either, Uncle, Dale, I, United, Airlines 2. Our new address is 100 N. Link Ave., Wichita, Kansas.*

*NOTE: Although abbreviations are not acceptable in formal writing, they have been included for practice.

3. A. You're B. their 4. higher**

**NOTE: This is a good place to review the concept of "than I". <u>I</u>, and not <u>me</u>, is correct because <u>jump</u> has been deleted.

5. AMV/RA: While the children made sand castles on the beach, the teenagers played volleyball. At the beach, the children made sand castles, and the teenagers played volleyball.

DAY 124: 1. Is, Babe, Ruth's, Baseball, Hall, Fame, Cooperstown 2. I. Mountain chains / A. Rockies / B. Appalachians / II. Rivers / A. Colorado / B. Rio Grande 3. I, he, she, we, they, you, it, who 4. fragment (no verb) 5. AMV/RA: The blue flowered pillow case is torn. The torn pillow case is blue-flowered.

DAY 125: 1. A, Acadia, National, Park, Maine 2. Dr. Tarn and his wife went to an A.M.A. meeting July 21, 1970, in Ohio. 3. him (with him) 4. better 5. AMV/RA: Joyce is a gymnast whose specialty is tumbling. Joyce, a gymnast, specializes in tumbling.

DAY 126: 1. A, Lumbertown, U., S., A., Minnesota 2. "I like dancing better," replied Tom's friend. 3. A. ride(s), rode, (has/have/had) ridden B. do(es), did, (has/have/had) done C. take(s), took, (has/have/had) taken 4. Seven (Seven cows), hungry (hungry cows), the (the grass), green (green grass), leafy (leafy grass) 5. AMV/RA: When we went to the circus, we saw a lion jump through a ring. We saw a lion jump through a ring at the circus.

DAY 127: 1. A. "Old King Cole" B. The Velveteen Rabbit C. Eight Is Enough D. Where the Red Fern Grows 2. No, you're not taking Spencer's snake with you.(!) 3. A (A fox), quick (quick fox), brown (brown fox), the (the dog), lazy (lazy dog) 4. A. pets B. children C. moose D. recesses E. boxes F. memories 5. AMV/RA: Jeremy is riding on a blue rocking horse. The rocking horse on which Jeremy is riding is painted blue.

DAY 128: 1. Some Russian, White, House
2.
> 66 Lincoln Drive
> Whittier, CA 90607
> Sept. 22, 19--

> Dear Joan,
> Our twenty-one friends will be arriving in Tulsa, Oklahoma, in October.

> Sincerely,
> Marsha

3. A. heading B. greeting (salutation) C. message (body) D. closing E. signature 4. stolen; should have stolen 5. AMV/RA: Whereas his father writes animal stories, his mother writes stories about cooking.

DAY 129: 1. A. "All Summer in a Day" B. The Merchant of Venice C. "Why Nobody Pets the Lion at the Zoo" D. "Stopping by Woods on a Snowy Evening" 2. Jody's brother, however, draws horses, cats, and dogs. 3. Chris's plates 4. is, am, are, was, were, be, being, been, has, have, had, do, does, did, may, must, might, shall, should, can, could, will, would 5. AMV/RA: The eight o'clock play will begin in ten minutes.

DAY 130: 1. According, <u>Genesis,</u> <u>Bible,</u> Jacob's, Joseph 2. A. "America the Beautiful" B. <u>The Wizard of Oz</u> C. <u>Tex</u> D. <u>Field and Stream</u> 3. eats 4. Recently (when) , in (where), out (where) 5. AMV/RA: Although the sky was blue in the morning, it rained in the afternoon. The sky was blue in the morning, but it rained in the afternoon.

DAY 131: 1. A, Hindu, New, Delhi, India 2. The company's address is P. O. Box 43, New York, N. Y. 3. A. Two B. there 4. The <u>secretary</u> ~~of the club~~ <u>has introduced</u> the treasurer. 5. AMV/RA: Penguins waddled across the snow and jumped into the water. Waddling across the snow, the penguins jumped into the water.*

*NOTE: Although this is a more complex sentence, students should be **taught** how to write it.

DAY 132: 1. The, Wabash, Travel, Agency, Alaskan 2. A. "Thirteen" B. <u>Sports Illustrated</u> C. <u>U. S. S. Constitution</u> 3. A. gloves B. Markin Theater C. Anderson House Restaurant D. movie theater 4. AMV/RA: Yeah!, Wow!, Oh! 5. AMV/RA: One of the six kitchen lights is burned out. Only five of the six kitchen lights are burning.

DAY 133: 1. A, Boston, Hilton, Hotel, May 2. A. <u>Our Family Tree</u> B. "I'm Nobody" C. "Bingo" D. <u>Gettysburg Times</u> 3. eventually (when), inside (where) 4. A. adjective (Those trees) B. pronoun 5. AMV/RA: The barbecued slices of turkey were placed in sandwiches. The turkey in the sandwiches had been sliced and barbecued.

DAY 134: 1. Their, Daytona, Goodyear, Company 2. Yes, you may read John's essay entitled "My Vacation." 3. and, but, or 4. **don**'t 5. AMV/RA: Jenny's friend, Lori, won a short story contest.* Jenny's friend who won the short story contest is Lori.

*This sentence may also read, "Jenny's friend Lori won a short story contest."

DAY 135: 1. A. <u>Freedom of Speech</u> B. <u>The Last of the Mohicans</u> C. "A Day to Remember" D. <u>The Days of Our Lives</u> 2. Our team, for example, scored thirty-one points. 3. lane (down the lane), corner (around the corner) 4. A. Uncle Kim and Aunt Edna's clock B. Farmer Jones's ducks C. our teacher's cards 5. AMV/RA: Their new car is gray with bucket seats and fancy wheels. Their new gray car has bucket seats and fancy wheels.

DAY 136: 1. Has, Attorney, Gill, Adams, County 2. One-half of Carl's grades were good, but he failed math. 3. A. we'll B. won't C. they're D. wouldn't E. she's F. haven't 4. well (adverb telling **how**) 5. AMV/RA: The misbehaving child threw herself on the floor and screamed. The child misbehaved by throwing herself on the floor and screaming.

DAY 137: 1.

11 Bow Lane
Phoenix, Arizona 85015
December 1, 19--

Dear Cousin Louie,
    I saw Disneyland last summer when visiting Anaheim,
California.

Sincerely yours,
Arnie T. Bogs

2. I believe, Mr. Dobbs, that you're the last entrant.(!) 3. she (subject = Mary and she) 4. leaves (<u>One</u> ~~of the girls~~ <u>leaves</u> ~~on Friday.~~) 5. AMV/RA: Although the clothes have been in the dryer for thirty minutes, they are still damp.

DAY 138: 1. Is, Vista, International, Hotel, Penn, Avenue, Pittsburgh 2. An ex-marine delivered a long, political speech. 3. A. adjective (that coat) B. pronoun 4. <u>sh</u>, <u>ch</u>, <u>s</u>, <u>x</u>, <u>z</u> 5. AMV/RA: The wrinkled shirts had been stuffed in a suitcase. The shirts were wrinkled because they had been stuffed in a suitcase. Having been stuffed in a suitcase, the shirts were wrinkled.*

*This is a more complex sentence; however, it can be taught.

DAY 139: 1. During, Ice, Age, Antarctic, Ocean 2. A. ft. B. lb. C. in. D. P.M. E. Rd. F. m* (*Note that there is no period after metric values.) 3. better 4. him (object of the preposition = him) 5. AMV/RA: After placing your name in the right corner of the paper, place the date below it. On the paper, place your name in the right hand corner and the date below it.

DAY 140: 1. At, Russell's, Tavern, Gettysburg, President, George, Washington 2. On Tuesday, June 6, 1940, my father's friend married. 3. A. concrete B. concrete C. abstract D. concrete E. abstract F. abstract 4. A. mustn't B. you'll C. I'd D. what's E. can't F. wouldn't 5. AMV/RA: Tad's blue racing bike was a birthday gift. Tad's blue bike, a racer, was a birthday gift.*

*NOTE: This is a more difficult concept.

DAY 141: 1. They, Swiss, English, Miracle, Market 2. Sophia said, "We're flying there, and we'll return by train." 3. Who's (Who's = Who is) 4. A. common B. common C. proper D. common E. common F. proper 5. AMV/RA: The old, gold coin is valuable. The valuable, gold coin is old.

DAY 142: 1. The, Jewish, Egypt, Moses 2. Ms. Davis asked, "Where's your car, Vicki?" 3. drunk; <u>must have drunk</u> 4. A. adjective (Many ribbons) B. pronoun (<u>Many</u> ~~of the flowers~~ <u>bloomed</u>.) 5. AMV/RA: Before crossing the street, the child looked both ways. The child first looked both ways and then crossed the street.

DAY 143: 1. A, Lutheran, Moon, Mountain 2. Dad's company is located at 42 Dee Rd., Atlanta, Georgia 30345. 3. I (You may need to teach the easy concept of inverting the sentence in order to "prove" the answer. "**I** was the winner." "**Me** was the winner." is incorrect.)

DAY 144: 1. A, Fair, Grounds, Smithsonian, Institution's, Renwick, Gallery 2. A gentle, cool breeze blew across the run-down sailboat. 3. A. run(s), ran, (has/have/had) run B. eat(s), ate, (has/have/had) eaten C. see(s), saw, (has/have/had) seen 4. well (adverb telling **how**) 5. AMV/RA: While water-skiing, the lady drove the boat and the man skied. During a water-skiing trip, the man skied while the lady drove the boat.

DAY 145: 1. The, Hopi, Indians, Southwest 2. The Hudson Riv. area of N. Y. is a lovely, fertile region*. 3. YOUR FIRST AND LAST NAME / YOUR STREET ADDRESS / CITY, STATE ZIP 4. Mandy, pens, pencils, notebook 5. AMV/RA: June's present was wrapped in blue paper with a white bow. The present with blue paper and a white bow is a gift for June.

*NOTE: As previously stated, abbreviations in formal writing should be avoided. However, abbreviations are used here for practice.

DAY 146: 1. A, Biglerville, Memorial, Hospital, Tuesday 2. It's raining today, and I've, without a doubt, forgotten my umbrella. 3. dog 4. The plumber in the red hat talked and fixed our faucet. 5. AMV/RA: Jim's sunglasses are on the tiled counter.

DAY 147: 1. Last, Captain, Doug, Bayn, Astrodome, Houston 2. "I love it!" exclaimed Nikki. 3. A horse ate an apple. (Direct object = apple) 4. A. two B. their C. hear 5. AMV/RA: Lori and her grandmother took a trip to England. Lori went with her grandmother to England.

DAY 148: 1. The, Senator, Gert, San, Francisco 2. The bright, shining light cast its glow on the ex-marine's car. 3. A. dishes B. friends C. sheep D. classes E. children F. mothers-in-law 4. more eager (comparing two) 5. AMV/RA: The friendly St. Bernard often jumps over the fence. The St. Bernard who is friendly often jumps over the fence.

DAY 149: 1. The, Snow, White, Seven, Dwarfs, Tri-Theater** 2. Mary's dad, her uncle, and her cousin went to Bangor, Maine, yesterday. 3. fall (The barrels in the arena fall over.) 4. any 5. AMV/RA: Janis's bicycle was in the school's driveway. The bicycle that's in the school driveway belongs to Janis.

**NOTE: The rule states that in a hyphenated title, both words are capitalized.

DAY 150: 1. Does, March, Dimes, Association, Easter 2. Two-thirds of the class went to Brian's party. 3. their (antecedent = trees) 4. First (when), outside (where), afterwards (when) 5. AMV/RA: Ms. Sax is repairing the broken copy machine that has a paper jam. The broken copy machine with jammed paper is being repaired by Ms. Sax.

DAY 151: 1. Is, Tournament, Roses, Parade, Pasadena 2. Because dinner wasn't prepared, we didn't leave until 7:00 P.M. 3. A. sets B. laid 4. Sal wants to go* ~~with Jerry and me~~. 5. AMV/RA: While one hamster in the cage drinks water, the other one darts around. Although one hamster is darting around the cage, the other one is drinking water.

*NOTE: **to go** = infinitive (not a prepositional phrase)

DAY 152: 1. A, Christian, Christ's, Bethlehem 2. No, I don't believe that June 1, 1919, is the answer. 3. Boldly (how), inside (where), very (to what extent) 4. Martha's**, friend, chef, resort, house 5. AMV/RA: Jane left the room in angry silence. Leaving the room, Jane was angry and silent.

**NOTE: Martha's is a possessive noun; however, some would argue that Martha's is a possessive noun used as an adjective.

DAY 153: 1. An, Dr., Lang, Smith, Medical, Building 2. A. Suzanne B. Titanic C. "Writing" D. The Owl 3. A. buy(s), bought, will (shall) buy B. dance(s), danced, will (shall) dance 4. AMV/RA: No! Fabulous! Wow! Yeah! 5. AMV/RA: Dr. Jobe is a veterinarian who vaccinates our cows. Dr. Jobe, a veterinarian, vaccinates our cows.

DAY 154: 1. The, Sierra, Madre, Mountains, West 2. "Yeah! Our team scored twenty-five points!" exclaimed Aaron. 3. I 4. Each ~~of the dancers~~ performed and then bowed. 5. AMV/RA: Daren, who is a tumbler, competes in state tournaments and often wins. Daren, a tumbler, competes in state tournaments and often wins.

DAY 155: 1. Does, Professor, Kelly, English 2. A. Fiddler on the Roof B. Japan's People C. "Your Hair" D. "Evangeline" 3. YOUR STREET ADDRESS / CITY, STATE ZIP / DATE 4. A. adverb B. preposition (up the stairs) 5. AMV/RA: The lady in the grocery store screamed because her purse had been stolen. The lady screamed that her purse had been stolen.

DAY 156: 1. Later, Judge, Worth, U., S., Capitol 2. Phil asked, "Where's the non-fiction book, Greg?" 3. AMV/RA: love, hope, gentleness, grief, truth 4. Two (Two ladies), young (young ladies), that (that boat), sinking (sinking boat) 5. AMV/RA: Doug's brother is working as a waiter at a newly-opened restaurant. Doug's brother, a waiter, works at a restaurant that just opened.

DAY 157: 1. During, Orient, Sam, Great, Wall, China 2. Her ex-boyfriend works and attends college. 3. fragment 4. A. heading B. greeting (salutation) C. message (body) D. closing E. signature 5. AMV/RA: The stained, wooden floors need to be sanded. The floors that are wooden and stained need to be sanded.

DAY 158: 1./2.

2 Cree Street
Glendale, Arizona 85306
July 3, 19--

My dear aunt,

    Let's meet in Picadilly Square in London, England, in May.

Your niece,
Tonya

3. always (when), here (where), when (when) 4. Brett and Tina's fountain 5. AMV/RA: After three hours of hiking into a canyon, the group ate lunch.

DAY 159: 1. Did, Captain, Jones, President, Camp, David 2. An airplane called the Spruce Goose is at Long Beach, California, I believe. 3. hours (within two hours), ankle (of the ankle) 4. A. command (imperative) B. statement (declarative) C. question (interrogative) 5. AMV/RA: Although Martha talks loudly, Martha's sister is very quiet. Martha talks loudly, but her sister is very quiet.

DAY 160: 1. A, Germany, Lincoln, Memorial, U., S., Senate 2. The U.S.S. Constitution in Boston, Massachusetts, is historical. 3. A. their B. Too C. hear 4. A. lie(s), lay, (has/have/had) lain B. start(s), started, (has/have/had) started 5. AMV/RA: Sherry purchased a bag of unsalted popcorn. Sherry purchased unsalted popcorn in a bag.

DAY 161: 1. A, Lakewood, Middle, School 2. Three-fourths of Laura's friends, I think, were there.
3. / 4._____

    YOUR FIRST AND LAST NAME
    YOUR STREET ADDRESS
    CITY, STATE   ZIP

YOUR FRIEND'S FIRST AND LAST NAME
YOUR FRIEND'S STREET ADDRESS
CITY, STATE   ZIP

_____
5. AMV/RA: Dark clouds rolled in, and rain fell for an hour. After dark clouds rolled in, rain fell for an hour.

DAY 162: 1. The, French, Opoe, Store, Cherry, Valley 2. Sandy's car, her bike, and her dog are in the family's garage. 3. race 4. A. common B. common C. proper D. common E. common F. proper 5. AMV/RA: The white speeding car is dented. The white dented car was speeding.

DAY 163: 1. At, Delgado's, Pizza, House, Italian 2. A. <u>How to Eat Fried Worms</u> B. "The Gift of the Magi" C. <u>Annie</u> D. "Daisy" 3. A. noun B. pronoun C. pronoun D. noun E. pronoun F. noun 4. Yesterday (when), down (where), so (to what extent), gently (how) 5. AMV/RA: Because a brush fire is burning, the air is filled with smoke. A brush fire is burning and filling the air with smoke.

DAY 164: 1. After, Ice, Age, Asian, Bering, Strait 2. Mr. and Mrs. Jacobs sell the following: yogurt, ice cream, and milk. 3. A. lie(s), lay, (has/have/had) lain B. smile(s), smiled, (has/have/had) smiled C. see(s), saw, (has/have/had) seen D. grow(s), grew, (has/have/had) grown 4. myself, himself, herself, yourself, ourselves, themselves, itself 5. AMV/RA: Before lunch, they shopped at a new mall and bought sweaters. Shopping at a new mall before lunch, they bought sweaters.

DAY 165: 1. When, Harold's, Europe, Eiffel, Tower, Leaning, Tower, Pisa, Swiss 2. "Wow! He's enclosed one-half of Ralph's collection!" exclaimed Judy. 3. A. abstract B. concrete C. abstract D. abstract E. concrete F. concrete*
    *Although one can argue that air is not actually seen, it can be broken down into
      visible molecules.
4. Who?, What?, Which?, Whose? 5. AMV/RA: Even though a security guard searched the parking lot for a stolen wallet, he did not find it. The security guard searched the parking lot for a stolen wallet, but it was not found.

DAY 166: 1. For, Canadian, Kellogg's, Danish 2. The answer, I think, isn't twenty-three, Lois. 3. A. pronoun B. adjective (both adults) 4. A. rise(s), rose, will (shall) rise B. draw(s), drew, will (shall) draw C. dance(s), danced, will (shall) dance 5. AMV/RA: No one helped the lady wash her new car. The lady, herself, washed the new car.

DAY 167: 1. Mrs., R., Dil, Hindu, Santa, Ana, College 2. "No, Lee, we aren't," said Tara, "leaving for Boise, Idaho, today." 3. A. painters' meeting B. oxen's master C. Chris's sofas D. vase's color 4. closer (2) 5. AMV/RA: While Sandy watched television, Jana and Gregory drew pictures. Sandy watched television, and Gregory and Jana drew pictures.

DAY 168: 1. Is, Fingal's, Cave, Staffa, Island, Scotland 2. Although two-fifths of the children didn't go, the picnic was fun. 3. The (The sundae), large (large sundae), walnut (walnut sundae), a (a tray), round (round tray), silver (silver tray) 4. A. well, better, best B. hard, harder, hardest C. eagerly, more eagerly, most eagerly 5. AMV/RA: Because no one has watered the grass nor has it rained recently, the grass is brown. The brown grass is a result of no watering and no recent rainfall.

DAY 169: 1. The, Methodist, Brown, Street, Bible 2. When the team had won, the coaches' treat was pizza and coke. 3. A. dashes B. calves C. rings D. lice E. brothers-in-law F. cries 4. A. fragment B. sentence 5. AMV/RA: Although his blue lunch box is shaped like a radio, it doesn't play music. His blue lunch box shaped like a radio doesn't play music.

DAY 170: 1. In, Spanish, Inca, Indians, Peru 2. Were you, by the way, born Jan. 30, 1980, in Toledo, Ohio? 3. children's pig 4. A. fragment B. sentence C. fragment D. sentence (subject = you understood) 5. AMV/RA: Joel made a paper airplane and flew it across the room. Having made a paper airplane, Joel flew it across the room.

DAY 171: 1. During, American, Revolution, Tory, Party, England 2. Yes, her well-mannered nephew arrived on the Icelandic. 3. long 4. AMV/RA: Oh! Wow! Drat! 5. AMV/RA: Myra joined an expensive fitness center yesterday. Although the fitness center that opened yesterday is expensive, Myra joined.

DAY 172: 1. Because, James, Madison's, U., S., Constitution, Father, Constitution 2. "You're the best," the man announced, "in this division." 3. A. had **lain** B. might have **sneaked** C. Has **brought** D. Should have **seen** 4. One ~~of the children~~ ran ~~to the gate~~ and opened it. 5. AMV/RA: The bicyclist stopped and rested on a park bench.

DAY 173: 1. In, Canton, Ohio, Pro, Football, Hall, Fame 2. Jenny asked, "Where's Jessica's note pad?" 3. is, am, are, was, were, be, being, been, has, have, had, do, does, did, may, must, might, shall, should, will, would, can, could 4. and, but 5. AMV/RA: The engraved, silver belt buckle belongs to a rancher. The rancher's silver belt buckle is engraved.

DAY 174: 1. Duane, Fort, Ticonderoga, American, Revolution 2. "You're right," the clerk said, "and I'll exchange it." 3. not, so, very, too, quite, rather, somewhat 4. A. doesn't B. we'll C. who's D. can't E. won't F. I've 5. AMV/RA: Joe purchased gum drops, licorice, and crackers at the drugstore. When Joe walked to the drugstore, he purchased gum drops, licorice, and crackers.

DAY 175: 1. A, German, Moby, Dick 2. When Barb's uncle visits, he often brings pasta, bread, or sausage. 3. most slowly (comparing three) 4. Those (Those winners), happy (happy winners), large (large trophies), gold (gold trophies) 5. AMV/RA: Mrs. Delany is cooking a turkey in an oblong roasting pan. Mrs. Delany's turkey is being roasted in an oblong pan.

DAY 176: 1. The, Cann, Dutch 2. A. "Insects" B. <u>My Backyard</u> C. "Super Jaws" D. <u>Come Follow Me</u> E. "Hickory Dickory Dock" 3. A. adjective (this direction) B. pronoun 4. well (adverb telling **how**) 5. AMV/RA: Although Millie's first answer of five was incorrect, her second answer was right. Millie's first answer of five was incorrect, but her second answer was correct.

DAY 177: 1. During, Hawaiian, Polynesian, Waikiki, Beach 2. "I think," said Marion, "that your shoe is untied." 3. ~~Throughout the day~~, squirrels <u>rushed</u> in and out ~~among the trees~~. 4. <u>We</u> <u>ate</u> doughnuts and <u>drank</u> juice ~~for breakfast~~. DIRECT OBJECTS = doughnuts, juice 5. AMV/RA: Salco Industries on Porter Avenue makes car mirrors. Salco Industries, located on Porter Avenue, makes car mirrors.

DAY 178: 1. A. <u>If There Were Dreams to Sell</u> B. "A Million and One Wishes" C. "An Apple for Colliwobble" D. "Barry Has a Fright" E. "The Boy Who Chased After a Cow" * (*Prepositions of five or more letters are capitalized in titles.) 2. Janice's sister left Nashville, Tennessee, yesterday. 3. YOUR STREET ADDRESS / CITY, STATE ZIP / DATE / Tatum Company / 12 Mission Bay Drive / San Diego, California 92109 4. door, house, patio 5. AMV/RA: The street sweeper that came today was driven by my friend's grandpa.

DAY 179: 1. His, Uncle, Gil, Arabian, Santa, Fe, New, Mexico 2. Hasn't the girls' swimming team returned, Miss Hart? 3. lain; <u>had lain</u> 4. A. exclamation (exclamatory) B. question (interrogative) C. command (imperative) D. statement (declarative) 5. AMV/RA: Please pick up the bird book that is on the floor. A book about birds is on the floor; please pick it up.**

  **You may wish to review the use of semicolon.

DAY 180: 1. / 2.

Brak Lane
Chelsea, MI or Mi. 48118
Dec. 12, 19--

My very good friend,
  We're looking forward to visiting Shelter Island, the zoo, and a Mexican food restaurant.

Your pal,
Shelly L. Jabbel

3. A. heading B. greeting (salutation) C. message (body) D. closing E. signature 4. me, him, her, us, them, you, it, whom 5. AMV/RA: While Taley's parents went to Ohio, Taley stayed with her aunt.

Pura Dignam 1994

La abuelita y su casa de muñecas

por MaryLou M. Smith

Ilustraciones de Ann Blackstone

SCHOLASTIC INC.

New York Toronto London Auckland Sydney

 A Ann Marie Bottoms,
muchísimas gracias.

Grandmother's Adobe Dollhouse
La abuelita y su casa de muñecas

Text copyright © 1984 by MaryLou M. Smith.
Spanish translation copyright © 1993 by Scholastic Inc.
All rights reserved. Published by Scholastic Inc.,
730 Broadway, New York, NY 10003, by arrangement
with New Mexico Magazine.
Printed in the U.S.A.
ISBN 0-590-47489-8
ISBN 0-590-29197-1 (meets NASTA specifications)

1 2 3 4 5 6 7 8 9 10   08   00 99 98 97 96 95 94

Muchas de las cosas que hay en la casa de muñecas de mi abuelita todavía conservan el mismo nombre que les dieron los habitantes mexicanos y españoles de Nuevo México hace muchos años. Esos nombres aparecen en el texto en letra negrita.

Mi abuelita vive en Nuevo México. A ella le encantan las casas de muñecas y todas las cositas que se les pone dentro. Mi favorita es su casita de muñecas de adobe. Cuando mi abuelita y yo jugamos con su casita de adobe, me cuenta muchas cosas sobre Nuevo México.

Mi abuelita hizo su casita de muñecas igual a una casa de adobe de verdad. Recorrió todo Nuevo México coleccionando cosas en miniatura para ponerle dentro.

Ella dice que en el mundo no hay otras casas como las de adobe de Nuevo México. Me cuenta que las hicieron con sus propias manos los primeros habitantes de Nuevo México: los indígenas pueblo y navajo, los colonos españoles, así como los colonos anglosajones y mexicanos. ¡Son muchas manos!

Déjenme que les enseñe la casita de adobe de mi abuela y entenderán lo que digo.

Síganme, pero caminen de puntillas con mucho cuidado sobre las yemas de los dedos. Imaginemos que medimos solamente tres pulgadas. Las cosas que miden un pie en una casa de verdad, miden sólo una pulgada en la casa de muñecas de mi abuelita.

¿Ven la tira de chiles que se está secando afuera, colgada de la puerta de enfrente? Mi abuelita la llama **ristra**. Cada vez que veo una ristra, se me antoja arrancar uno de esos chiles de brillante color rojo y comérmelo. Pero mi abuelita dice que son tan picantes que me quemarían la lengua.

Tenemos que esperar a que los chiles se sequen. Entonces ella molerá uno para condimentar las enchiladas de la cena. No me

importa esperar, ¡pues las enchiladas de mi abuelita son deliciosas!

Antes de entrar, les voy a dar algunos datos sobre el **adobe.** Ésta casa y todas las casas de adobe de Nuevo México en realidad estan hechas de barro.

Los pueblo hacían sus casas de barro hace mucho, mucho tiempo. Con sus propias manos, moldeaban el barro para hacer las paredes de sus casas.

Cuando los españoles llegaron a Nuevo México, comenzaron a hacer ladrillos de barro y a colocarlos uno sobre otro para construir paredes.

Para hacer una casa de adobe, primero hay que encontrar un terreno arcilloso y sacar arcilla. La arcilla se mezcla con agua y se revuelve, como haciendo tortas de barro. También hay que añadirle un poco de paja para evitar que se agriete al secarse.

Después se echa la arcilla en moldes de madera y se empareja. Los ladrillos así formados se ponen a secar bajo el brillante sol de Nuevo México hasta que estén duros. Una vez secos, se podrán construir casas con ellos.

Yo nunca he hecho ladrillos de adobe pero me parece que necesitaría un amigo o una amiga que me ayudara. ¿Quieren que lo probemos algún día?

Ahora que estamos dentro, ¿no les gustaría verlo todo a la vez?

Miren hacia arriba. ¿Ven el techo de maderitas? Se llaman **latillas** y en realidad son ramitas de árboles.

Los maderos redondos se llaman **vigas** y sostienen el techo de adobe.

¿Ven cómo las latillas se colocan entre las vigas primero en una dirección y luego en la otra? Mi abuela dice que parecen espinas de pescado. Me gusta la forma en que las latillas se ajustan una a la otra.

Los bloques tallados que ven al final de cada viga se llaman "ménsulas". ¿No es cierto que hacen que las puntas de las vigas se vean muy bien acabadas? A veces las ménsulas son sencillas; otras veces son muy trabajadas.

Más tarde, cuando volvamos a salir, no se olviden de mirar arriba por los lados de la casa. Verán como las vigas sobresalen de las paredes de adobe.

Uno de los libros de mi abuelita dice que los pueblo fueron los primeros en hacer vigas que sobresalían de esa manera. Los troncos con los que hacían las vigas no siempre se ajustaban a la medida, así que los dejaban sobresalir de las paredes. ¿No les parece una manera muy ingeniosa de resolver el problema?

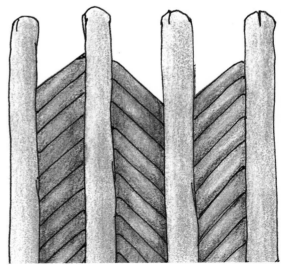

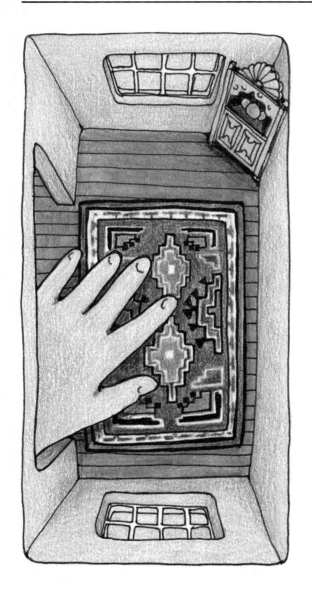

Ahora miren hacia abajo, debajo de sus dedos.

¿No les parece increíble que alguien pudiera hacer a mano diseños tan bellos en una alfombra tan pequeñita? Mi abuelita viajó al norte de Nuevo México para conocer a la artesana que hizo esta pequeña alfombra. Es una señora navajo y tejió esta alfombrita con el mismo diseño de las frazadas que su gente ha hecho durante muchos años.

Primero esquilan las ovejas que crían, luego hilan la lana en estambres y por último la tejen en telares verticales.

A este tipo de alfombra se le llama de "Dos colinas grises". Un día traté de encontrar las colinas grises y mi abuelita me dijo que "Dos colinas grises" es el nombre de la tienda que queda cerca del lugar donde se hacen las alfombras. ¡Ahí es donde están las dos colinas grises!

Las alfombras de "Dos colinas grises" se reconocen por sus colores. Para hacerlas, los navajo tejen la lana tal y como la cortan de las ovejas, sin pintarla.

Algunas ovejas son negras, otras blancas. Los diferentes tonos de marrón que se ven en sus alfombras provienen de las ovejas de color café.

Me gusta cerrar los ojos e imaginarme a los pastores navajo caminando por esas colinas grises y cuidando a sus ovejas de muchos colores.

Vamos a la cocina, que allí hay muchas cosas que quiero mostrarles.

Cierren los ojos y abran la m a n o. ¿V e n e s t o s **chiles** v e r d e s pequeñitos? Los tomé de esa repisa de mosaico. Son como los chiles de verdad que comemos en casi todas las comidas en casa de mi abuelita.

Seguramente piensan que los chiles verdes son muy, muy picantes, pero mi abuelita dice que hay muchas variedades de chiles. Ella compra los que no son picantes para mí.

A veces me deja que la ayude a asarlos en el horno hasta que se cubren de burbujitas color café. Luego los metemos rápidamente en agua fría. Después de pelar la piel quemada, vemos que siguen siendo verdes.

Mi abuelita rellena los chiles con pedacitos de queso mientras yo bato los huevos. Luego, cuando todos tenemos hambre, reboza los chiles en el huevo y los fríe en aceite caliente.

Yo me apresuro a llegar a la mesa, donde todos están esperando. ¡No quiero perderme esos chiles!

¿Ven esas mazorcas de maíz en la canastita? En algunas partes las llaman "maíz indio". Me sorprendió mucho descubrir que el maíz puede ser azul, café y hasta rojo. Mi favorito es el que tiene granos color café y amarillo en la misma mazorca.

Mi abuelita dice que hoy en día ese maíz sólo se usa para decorar las cocinas. A veces se cuelga de la pared y otras veces se coloca en canastas. Para cocinar se usan otras variedades modernas de maíz.

Pero a mí me gustaría cocinar con ese maíz. Podríamos intentar hacer el **pozole** de mi abuelita. ¿Lo han probado alguna vez?

Lo mejor del pozole es su rico olor cuando uno entra en la casa. Se hace con maíz cacahuazintle. Antes tenían que hacerlo de maíz que había sido remojado en lejía, pero ahora mi abuelita lo compra en la tienda, empacado. Lo encuentra al lado de los paquetes de chiles rojos secos.

Primero se remoja el maíz en agua y luego se cocina con cerdo, chiles rojos y mucho ajo y cebolla. Me gusta el pozole. Abuelita me deja meter la tortilla en el plato y así no me pierdo ni una gota.

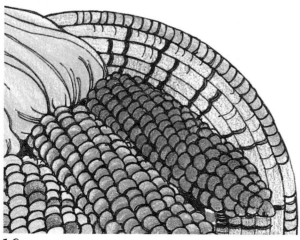

¿Han visto alguna vez una cama en la cocina? Bueno, pues miren en esa esquina. La chimenea tiene por encima un anaquel de madera que se llama "cama de pastor". También se llama "chimenea de pastor".

Cuando mi abuelita me dijo que los pastores solían dormir sobre ese anaquel, pensé que bromeaba. Pero es cierto: el fuego de la chimenea les daba calor.

En realidad, cualquiera podría dormir ahí, pero más bien se usaba para secar chiles, calabazas y otros alimentos.

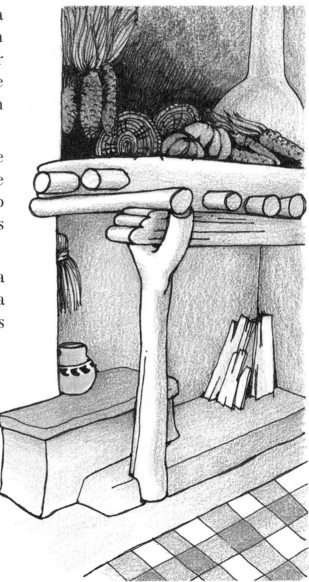

¿Tienen sed? Imaginémonos que esas **ollas** tan bonitas que están cerca de la ventana están llenas de agua. Así las llamaban los españoles.

Abuelita dice que los pueblo hicieron las ollas para acarrear agua. Las mujeres podían llevar esas ollas sobre la cabeza sin sostenerlas con las manos.

Las ollas se hacen con tiras de arcilla que parecen serpientes largas y regordetas enrolladas. Luego se emparejan con tanto cuidado que nadie creería que alguna vez parecían serpientes enrolladas. Mi abuela dice que toma mucho tiempo emparejarlas y que los pueblo lo hacen con calma.

¿Ven los diferentes diseños que les pintan por fuera? Cada aldea o pueblo tiene sus colores y diseños propios.

Dibujan los diseños con pinceles hechos con las fibras de la planta de la yuca y hacen los colores con las plantas y minerales que encuentran a su alrededor.

¿Saben lo que me dijo mi abuela acerca de los diseños de color negro de estas ollas? Que fueron pintados con una especie de miel muy espesa sacada de una planta que crece en las montañas Rocosas. Los indígenas hierven los ramos en agua y hacen una pintura que parece regaliz negro.

Abuelita me promete que algún día ella y yo vamos a tratar de hacer ollas de barro. Quizás hasta intentemos hacer nuestra propia pintura. ¿Les gustaría ayudarnos?

Volvamos a la sala. Tengo muchas cosas que enseñarles ahí. Esta chimenea se llama "chimenea de Santa Fe". Es de adobe, como las paredes.

Miren, incluso algunos de los muebles de la casita son de barro. Estos asientos se llaman **bancos.** Se pueden colocar a lo largo de las paredes si son rectos o en los rincones si son curvos.

Los huecos que ven en la pared encima de la chimenea se hicieron cuando construyeron las paredes de adobe. Mi abuelita los llama **nichos.**

Me gusta la forma de los bancos, los nichos y la chimenea, parecen haber sido hechos del mismo pedazo de adobe.

¿Les gustan las muñecas tanto como a mí? Bueno, mi abuela tiene muñecas de barro. Si tenemos mucho cuidado nos dejará tocarlas.

¿Ven a todos esos niñitos acurrucados encima de su abuelito? Algunos están trepados en su regazo, otros sobre sus piernas y algunos hasta sobre sus hombros. Mi abuelita dice que es un **cuentero.** Cada cuentero es diferente, pero todos tienen la boca abierta porque están cantando.

Los indígenas pueblo cochiti hicieron los cuenteros de mi abuelita. ¿No les parece que los niños se ven felices? Me recuerdan como me siento yo cuando mi abuelita me dice:—Matt, ven a sentarte en mi regazo para que te cuente un cuento.

Esta estatuilla está hecha de madera. Se le llama **bulto**. Los bultos son figuras religiosas talladas que hicieron los colonos españoles cuando llegaron a Nuevo México hace muchos años.

Algunas veces, las figuras religiosas están pintadas sobre madera. Entonces se les llama **retablos.** ¿Vieron el que está en el rincón encima de los bancos?

Tanto los retablos como los bultos son **santos**. Los hábiles talladores y pintores que los hacen se llaman **santeros**.

Me alegro de que abuelita tenga a su cuentero y a su bulto bien guardados en sus nichos.

Ahora vamos arriba. ¡A que les gano!

¡Cuántas chimeneas hay en esta casa! La que está en el rincón de esta recámara se llama "chimenea panal". Esas chimeneas se parecen mucho a los hornos al aire libre en los que los pueblo hornean pan. Los españoles simplemente los metieron en sus casas y los usaron como chimeneas.

Este gabinete de madera se llama **trastero.** Aquí en la recámara sirve de armario para guardar la ropa, pero por lo general los trasteros están en la cocina para guardar en ellos los platos y otros utensilios de cocina.

Artesanos mexicanos llamados **carpinteros** vinieron a Nuevo México y construyeron trasteros y otros muebles de madera tallada. Mi abuelita dice que en aquella época, el mueble más preciado de una familia de Nuevo México era su trastero.

Me gusta imaginarme que el sol brilla a través de los pequeños vidrios de estas "puertas francesas". Le pregunté a mi abuelita si las puertas francesas venían de Francia. No me explicaba como una casa de adobe de Nuevo México tenía puertas como ésas.

Mi abuelita me explicó que las puertas francesas llegaron con los primeros colonos anglosajones. Cuando llegaron a Nuevo México echaban de menos los muebles de sus casas en el este del país, así que mandaron a traer las puertas, sillas y sofás a los que estaban acostumbrados. Algunos de esos muebles llegaron a Nuevo México en grandes trenes.

Si quieren abrir una de esas puertecitas, podemos salir.

Miren ahora dónde estamos. Éste es el **patio** de arriba.

En Navidad colocamos **luminarias** por todo el borde de este patio. Una amiga de mi abuelita que es del norte de Nuevo México las llama **farolitos**.

Las luminarias o farolitos son la cosa más extraordinaria que he visto en Nuevo México. Para hacerlas se llenan de arena bolsas de papel manila y se mete una vela en cada una. Cuando todas las velas se encienden, crean una bella escena navideña. Las luminarias de la casita de muñecas son foquitos en vez de velas. ¡Prender cerillos en una casa de muñecas sería peligroso!

Bueno, ahora que han visto la casita de adobe de mi abuelita, ¿qué parte les gustó más?

Hay poca gente que vive en casas como ésta, pero casi todas las casas tienen algunas de las cosas que han visto en esta casa de muñecas.

Nunca he visto una chimenea de pastor en ningún lado, salvo en la casa de muñecas de mi abuelita y en un museo de Santa Fe. Pero he visto muchas chimeneas panal, y mucha gente tiene ristras, cuenteros y ollas.

Espero que vuelvan y que su visita sea por más tiempo. La próxima vez, nos imaginaremos que pasamos la noche en la casita de muñecas de adobe de mi abuelita. Estoy seguro que para la cena nos hará chilitos verdes rellenos de queso.

Podríamos subirnos al regazo del cuentero, quien nos contaría un lindo cuento y cuando fuera la hora de irnos a dormir, ¡podríamos turnarnos para dormir en la chimenea del pastor!

Me encanta visitar a mi abuela en Nuevo México. Cuando llega la hora de partir, echo una última mirada por las ventanas de su casita de adobe. Y cuando nos alejamos en el auto, le digo adiós en silencio a todas las casas de adobe y a todas las cosas tan lindas que tienen dentro. ¡Adiós!

Posdata

MaryLou M. Smith es una escritora y editora originaria de Nuevo México, donde su familia ha residido desde hace cuatro generaciones. Ahora vive en Colorado con su esposo y sus dos niños.

Matt Smith, su hijo de seis años, es el niño que nos mostró la casa de muñecas de adobe de su abuela.

La abuelita es LaVerne Smith, quien vive en Roswell, Nuevo México, donde tiene una mueblería, hace casas de muñecas y colecciona miniaturas. Ha hecho y amueblado varias casas de muñecas de adobe.

Ann Blackstone es una dibujante y diseñadora gráfica que heredó de su familia de arquitectos el amor por las casas. Vive con su gato Callie en Colorado en una casa que tiene 108 años.